PSALMS/NOW

Psalms / Now

by
Leslie F. Brandt

with art by
Corita Kent

Publishing House
St. Louis   London

Concordia Publishing House, St. Louis, Missouri
Concordia Publishing House Ltd., London, E. C. 1
Copyright © 1973 Concordia Publishing House
Library of Congress Catalog Card No. 73-78103
ISBN 0-570-03230-X
Manufactured in the United States of America

PREFACE

I first read the Book of Psalms through at the age of ten. I don't remember what they said to me at that time, but in the ensuing years they often articulated my feelings and verbalized my prayers as a struggling saint. In the twentieth year of my ministry I began to "rewrite" a few of them for my church bulletin. These were eventually published in three small volumes. PSALMS/NOW includes the collection of the three volumes and presents prayers or meditations on all 150 Psalms of the Old Testament.

I have tried to express what these Psalms say to me and about me. It is just possible that they may reveal to other readers something about themselves and give them a means of expressing their actual feelings in their conversations with God. These offerings are by no means an attempt to be scholarly or textual. On the other hand, they ought to indicate something of the honesty and humanity of the psalm-writers in their daily conflicts and to encourage us to be as honest in our pursuit of truth and our walk with God.

I am expressing what the psalmist might be saying if he were living in the twentieth century. It is true that the Christ name is not used; the word "Gospel" is not included; the Messianic import of the Psalms is not noted. Yet these prayers are those of the Christian on this side of the Easter event—one whose every approach to God must be by way of God revealed through Jesus Christ.

Today's Christian, like the ancient psalmist, can honestly and openly express his doubts and perplexities to his loving God. At the same time he can lay claim to God's promises and demonstrate his faith in celebration of His presence in the world today. While his doubts resolve into joy and celebration, he acknowledges God's ownership and commission for his life and dedicates himself to service.

If these psalm-writing efforts serve to make the ancient psalms more relevant for modern saints and if they may help to express more adequately the perpetual conflicts of a child of God in our complex society, they will serve their purpose.

Leslie F. Brandt

I

The man who chooses to live a significant life
    is not going to take his cues
      from the religiously indifferent.
Nor will he conform to the crowd
    nor mouth his prejudices
    nor dote on the failures of others.

His ultimate concern is the will of God.
He makes his daily decisions in respect to such.
He can be compared to a sturdy tree
    planted in rich and moist soil.
As the tree yields fruit,
    so his life manifests blessing for others.
His life is productive and effective.

This is not true concerning the ungodly.
They are like sand in a desert storm
    or leaves in an autumn wind.
They cannot stand against the judgments
    of the eternal God.
And they are most uncomfortable
    among those who demonstrate genuine faith
      in the God of righteousness.

The children of God walk in the course
    that God has ordained.
The children of unbelief walk
    in paths of self-destruction.

2

Why is it that dictators and governments
     throughout our world
  persist in persecuting
    the people of God?
They may be divided in everything else,
    but they unite in their endeavors
      to free themselves from the restraints of religion.

Disconcerting as this is to me,
    our great God laughs at their foolish efforts.
And His laughter will have the sound of fury
    in the day He determines to act against them.
He will reveal to them who truly is Lord and King.

But to me, even in the midst of my consternation,
    He speaks as a loving Father.
"You are My son and servant," He says.
"Trust in Me; the destiny of the world
    is in your hands.
You shall be the overcomer;
    you shall frustrate their attempts to destroy you."

So wise up, you who sit in high places.
Begin serving the God you are trying to silence.
Bow your hearts in submission
    before He crowns your heads with divine wrath.
Only those who rest in God's will
    are really secure.

3

O God, the obstacles that confront me today are so many!
And even as they press in upon me,
>> there are people about me
>>> who laugh at my childlike dependence on You.
They claim that my faith is futile,
>> that God is not interested in my petty problems.

But, God, You have surrounded me with Your love.
You envelop me with concern
>> and undergird me with grace.
When I reach out for You,
>> You are close enough to hear and to respond.

Whether I am awake or asleep,
>> You are near to me and will watch over me.
I do not have to be afraid
>> of these problems that assail me.
The conflicts of my life will not separate me from You.

I constantly seek Your deliverance
>> from all that hurts or hinders.
You are able to rid my life of everything
>> that may threaten my relationship to You.
You will in Your own good time set me free
>> from every human fault and frailty.
But even while I seek Your ultimate deliverance,
>> help me to sense Your presence and power
>>> in the midst of my many conflicts.

4

Dear God, respond to Your servant in distress;
  make room for a disciple in despair;
  listen to the agonizing cries of a child
    who is depressed and unhappy.

O you who I thought were my friends,
  why do you keep hacking at me,
    gloating over my errors, rejoicing at my failures,
    always looking for the very worst in me?

I must remember that I truly do belong to God,
  that He does feel for me when I hurt.

Go ahead, explode, blow up;
  it doesn't frighten God
    as long as it doesn't hurt anyone else.
But then, O foolish heart, simmer down,
  and begin renewing your confidence in God.

I hear voices about me
  whining about the wickedness of the world,
    begging for divine demonstration of might and right.
And yet I know I have discovered
  more delight in my relationship to You
  than they in all their possessions and pleasures.

And so I can lie down and sleep in peace.
Because of You, I am eternally secure.

5

Can You hear, O God, what I have to say?
Do You feel something of what I feel this morning?

I know, O God, that You are grieved
        by the selfishness of Your children.
The world You created seems to be falling apart.
Your creatures are living for themselves alone.
They are proud and self-sufficient.
They think they don't need You any longer.
I also know, O Lord, that I cannot exist
        without the assurance of Your eternal love.
Thus I commit myself once more to You and Your purposes.
Help me to walk in Your path for my life.
Give me grace to overcome the many obstacles in the way.

The philosophies that come out of our world
        bear little resemblance
            to the truth You revealed to us.
They are subtle and seductive, and men are led astray
        by forked tongues and suave soft-sell.
Enable us to recognize them for what they are:
        shallow, superficial, ultimately destructive.

Those who follow You need not be dismayed.
They can sing and dance in the joy of their Lord.
You will continue to reveal Yourself to them
        and care for them and work out Your purposes
            in and through them.

O God, don't clobber me in disgust
        or chastise me in anger.
But the fact is, I'm falling apart.
I am distraught and confused.
I am in deep trouble,
        and I don't know how long I can take it.

I can only beg You to enter into my conflict,
        to extricate me from its incessant battering,
        to demonstrate Your love
            in deliverance and salvation.
Otherwise I'm going down the drain;
        and how, then, could I either praise or serve You?

I am fed up with this continual agony;
        I can no longer endure these perpetual defeats.
I am becoming increasingly discouraged
        over my human frailties and fallibilities.

If only I could be sure
            that You know of my anguish,
            that You discern my cries for help,
            that You also feel and understand,
            that You will never let me go,
        then I could stand firm even in defeat
            and rise victorious even over my failures
            and make even my human weaknesses
                serve You.

7

O God, I come running to You
　　like a frightened child.
My pursuers, like hideous monsters,
　　seek to tear me limb from limb.

O Lord,
　　if I really am to blame for their hostilities,
　　if I have willfully hurt anybody,
　　if I have selfishly blighted another man's soul,
　　　then let the ax fall;
　　　I have no right to live;
　　　　I almost wish I could die.

O God, have mercy.
You know the secrets of my heart
　　and the desires of my flesh.
You know I want so much to do Your will.
You know my greatest enemy is myself,
　　how ineffectual I am
　　　in dealing with my inner conflicts.
You know, and You have assured me that You care.
You have judged my wickedness;
　　now rise up to deliver me
　　　from its ugly consequences.

Oh, when will there be an end to evil?
When will this frustrating struggle cease?
I claw like a wounded animal

at the promises of God for comfort,
    I appeal to His love for solace and strength.

I know the end of those
    who do not repent of their sins.
Their selfishness boomerangs; sin kicks back.
They stew in their own juice; they cut their own throats.

Thus I must persist in running to God in my defeats
    that I may learn to walk with Him in His victories.
I will continue to sing His praises
    and to lay claim to His righteousness.

8

+ [O God,

> how full of wonder and splendor You are!

I see the reflections of Your beauty
> and hear the sounds of Your majesty
>> wherever I turn.
Even the babbling of babes
> and the laughter of children
>> spell out Your name in indefinable syllables.]

+ [When I gaze into star-studded skies
> and attempt to comprehend the vast distances,
I contemplate in utter amazement
> my Creator's concern for me.
I am dumbfounded that You
> should care personally about me.]

And yet You have made me in Your image.
You have called me Your son.
You have ordained me as Your priest
And yet, and chosen me to be Your servant.
+ [You have assigned to me
> the fantastic responsibility
>> of carrying on Your creative activity.

O God,
> how full of wonder and splendor You are!]

Glory be ...

9

My heart overflows with gratitude to God.
I feel so exuberant
    I simply must express or explode.
I will give voice to my exultations;
    I will sing Your praises, O my God.

You helped me stand firm
    in spite of those who had it in for me,
and they were not successful
    in their efforts to discredit me.

You have destroyed great forces in history
    that rose up to oppose You.
You continue to rule over our fractured world,
    to sit in judgment over its nations and peoples.
You offer Your strong hand to those who are oppressed,
    Your loving concern to those who are troubled.
You never hide from those who seek You
    or forsake those who cling to You.

Sing the praises of God;
    proclaim loudly His deeds to the people.
For while He judges evildoers,
    He hears and remembers the cries of those in distress.

I need always Your gracious love.
You know all about my inner fears and doubts.
You hold me back from the brink of destruction.

You make it possible for me to sing Your praises
    and to rejoice in Your perpetual deliverance.
Ungodly nations sink in their own sewage.
Men who promote evil
        snare themselves in their own nets,
    but those who recognize their need of You
        shall be found by You.

Is it any wonder
    my heart overflows with gratitude to God?

10

Where in the world are You, O God?
Why do You run away when things go wrong?

The sensualist lives by the desires of the flesh.
The materialist seeks for temporal security alone.
The ungodly man indulges in self-worship;
      he assumes that "God is dead."

The point is, these are the ones who seem to prosper.
They laugh in scorn at those who are inclined toward piety.
They claim that they are in the driver's seat
      and cannot be dethroned.
They live and speak arrogantly and carelessly.
They are not concerned about the enslaved and the deprived.
They will take what they want
      irrespective of the hurt they cause others.

Wake up, O God! Come out of hiding!
How can You allow these God-defiers to get away with it?

O God, You do take note of those in conflict.
You will take account of the godless and the arrogant.
You are still Lord over all the world.
You do hear the cries of those who love You;
      You are perpetually concerned about their needs.
You will enable them to stand up
      against the oppression and pain of this life.

//

I am frightened by the insecurities about me.
I am sorely tempted to run for my life,
> to take refuge in foolish escapades
> > that dim the vision and drug the soul.

There is no escape
> from the realities of this fractured world.
When we awaken from our stupor
> or return to sobriety,
> they are ever present
> > to haunt and oppress us.

But there is a place of refuge.
God is in our midst.
He is aware of the fears and apprehensions
> of His beloved children.
He may not always rid us of our fears.
He does promise to face them with us,
> to make them stepping-stones to faith,
> to use them to draw us closer to Himself.

I need not worry overmuch
> about the distortions of this world.
I do need to be aware that God is here
> and allow Him through me
> > to reveal Himself to His world.

12

O God, help me.
The world is truly going to the dogs.
There is infidelity and deceit on all sides of me.
Every man seems to wear two faces.

And men even boast about their deeds of evil.
They assume that they can talk themselves
        out of any corner.
They defy authority and live for themselves alone.

Our God will not forever remain silent.
His voice like thunder will drown out
        the foolish boasts of His unfaithful creatures.
"The maligned and the deprived
        have suffered long enough," He will say.
"I will rise to their defense
        and grant them My protection."
And what God promises, He will do.

Keep us, great God, from the vile compromises
        and the rank complacency of this generation.

13

O God, sometimes You seem so far away.
I cannot in this moment sense Your presence
    or feel Your power.

The darkness about me is stifling.
This depression is suffocating.
How long, O God, do I have to live in this void?
O God, how long?

Break into this black night, O God;
    fill in this vast emptiness.
Enter into my conflict
    lest I fall never to rise again.

I continue to trust in Your ever-present love.
I shall again discover true joy
    in my relationship to You.
I will proclaim Your praises, my Lord,
    for You will never let me go.

14

How foolish it is to deny the existence of God
　　　or to say that "God is dead"!
And yet there are many who do so.
They say it in the way they live
　　　if not in the words they speak.

Our great God is forever searching for those
　　　who will open their lives to Him.
He is not looking for such
　　　in verbal professions alone
　　　　but in the way men live and act.

He sees denial and rebellion in the lives of all men.
What good they do is tainted by sin and self-centeredness.
They are more apt to be destructive than creative.
How foolish they are
　　　if they neglect to surrender their lives to God!

It is obvious that God works
　　　through those who trust Him,
　　　through those who dedicate their lives
　　　　to His service.
It is they who are set free from self-glory
　　　to enjoy and to serve the living God.
They can truly celebrate the eternal presence of God.

Who is the one, O Lord, that remains
    a part of Your kingdom?
What are the prerequisites
    for membership in Your family?

It is that one who walks circumspectly —
    and in obedience to Your precepts and principles.
He must be open and honest before God and man.
He must speak and act in love toward his neighbor.
He cannot condone that which is evil
    and must not participate
        in that which promotes injustice.
He must listen to his brother's griefs
    and complaints.
He must seek to lighten his burden
    and to share in his sorrow and pain.
He must reach out to heal rather than to hurt,
    to be kind and gentle to all who cross his path.

Those who lovingly relate to God and fellowman
    will never be separated from the family of God.

Sustain me, O God,
for I am anchoring my faith in You.
I say it again,
"You are my Lord;
when I am estranged from You,
I have nothing that is of any real worth."

The significant and contributive people
of this world
are those who know You.
They are the individuals I must respect.
Those who make lesser things their ultimate concern
are investing in eventual trouble and grief.
I cannot worship their idols
or respect their objectives.

I have chosen to make God my ultimate concern.
He is the Pilot of my ship.
Thus the course before me will lead
to ultimate fulfillment.
I am guaranteed an inheritance of infinite value.

I look to God as my chief counselor.
Even in the darkest of night
He is ready to teach and guide me.
I need only to recognize His perpetual presence.
Because He continually surrounds me,
I shall not lose my way.

Is it any wonder that I am happy?
Even my humanity, my tangible body,
    rests in the blessed realization of this security.
He will keep even my human self
    from the destructive clutch of evil.

You do show me the paths I must take.
Within Your all-embracing presence
    there is genuine fulfillment.
In my relationship with You
    I discover incomparable and eternal joy.

17

I cry to You out of desperation, my God.
Listen to me and judge me if I am in error.

I have honestly tried to do Your will,
        to promote Your causes, to speak Your Word.
I have avoided the pitfalls that have victimized
        so many about me.
I have acted in love rather than in anger.
I have never raised my hand in violence.
I have walked in the paths You have set before me.

And yet I am tripped up by despair.
There are great walls that I cannot break through,
        dead ends that lead nowhere,
        people to whom I cannot relate.
I reach out in concern and am rebuked with scorn.

I am weary, Lord, weary of well-doing.
I am tired of the reactions
        of those I seek to serve.
I seriously wonder if it is all worth it.

Grant me, O God, a measure of ecstasy.
Help me to feel good about myself
        and about my role in Your service.
Reveal Yourself in some special way this night
        that I may rest in joy and in peace.

It is no wonder that I love You, O God.
You have granted me a security
    that I could never find
        among the things of this world.

You have erased from my life the fear of death.
What follows the grave is not my fearful concern.
The traumatic experiences of this life
    cannot destroy me.
You are never out of reach
    but are ever aware of my problems and conflicts.

How great and all-powerful is my God!
The quaking of the earth,
    the shaking of the mountains,
    the blackness of the night,
    the beauty of the heavens,
    the lightning that crisscrosses our skies,
    the oceans that lash against our shores:
    this and much more bear witness
      to the majesty of my God.
And this is the God who is concerned about me.
He reaches into my distraught life
    to heal my wounds.
He encompasses me with eternal love.
He abides with me
    even in the midst of conflict or calamity.
He sets me free from self-idolatry

so I may serve His creatures about me.
He shields me from the forces that are intent
    on my destruction.
I am His delight and heart's desire.
It is no wonder, O God, that I love You.

Can there be any God but this God that I love?
He surrounds me with His strength
    and clothes me with His grace.
He puts into my hands gifts to relay to others.
He entrusts me with tasks
      far beyond my human abilities
    and enables me to carry them out.
He ordains me as His son and servant
    destined to accomplish His purposes
      amongst the peoples of this world.

It is thus that I celebrate God's presence
    in my life and world.
God is not dead; He lives.
I rejoice in His concern and love for me.
I will proclaim, O Lord,
    Your praises to anyone who will listen to me.
I will sing and shout and dance
    in the joy of knowing that You are my God.

19

Wherever I am, wherever I go,
    I can sense something of the power of God.
The grandeur of the mountains,
      the vastness of the oceans,
      the breathtaking wonder of interstellar space;
    all this proclaims the glory and majesty of God.
Even amid the clutter of our cities,
      built and abused by the hands of men,
    there are reflections of divine splendor.
Heaven's silence or earth's clamor
    may not be very articulate.
Yet God's voice can be heard.
He makes His presence known throughout the world.

God has made for man a path he is to walk in.
In His will there is order and purpose.
He has proclaimed and demonstrated eternal truth
    through the lips and lives of His children.
There are set before the sons of men
    precepts and principles which direct
      His creatures in the way of peace and joy.
He has given meaning to life,
    goal and objective to this existence.
Therein is the answer to man's inner need,
    the fulfillment of his deepest longings.
These things are more precious and of greater value
    than anything a man could ever experience
      or even dare to imagine.

31

This is the course which I must travel.
It is not easy; I make so many mistakes.
I am plagued with faults and obsessions.
O God, forbid that these should destroy me.
Set me free from their tenacious hold on me.
Encompass me with Your love and grace
    that these things may not stand
      between You and me.

O God,
    these are the thoughts
      that crowd my heart today.
Accept them and respond to them,
    and enable me to realize anew
      the security and serenity
        of Your loving presence in my life.

20

O my very dear friend,
How much I want to bear your burden,
    to share your trouble!
But I can only pray that God may be
      very close to you in your sorrow
    and keep you and protect you in your conflict.
May He remember that you are His own,
    that you have dedicated your life to Him,
    that your heart's desire is to serve and please Him.
May He reach out to touch you and heal you;
    may He fulfill your crying need in this hour.
And may we soon rejoice together over your deliverance
    and walk together in His service.

I know that God does stand by His own,
    that our failures do not stay His loving hand,
    that He can transform them into victories.
Men about us put their trust in rockets and computers,
    but such will fail to solve
      the real problems of our lives.
It is only in the name of God
    that we who fall can find the grace to rise again.

Hear my prayer on behalf of my friend, O God.
I want to share his defeat;
    may I also share in his victory.

21

O God,
> in the grace and strength that You daily grant,
>> Your servant finds reason for celebration.

You have truly fulfilled his innermost longings.
You have responded to his deepest needs.

He asked for security,
> and You encompassed him with love.

He looked to You for life,
> and You granted him life eternal.

He sought for identity,
> and You adopted him as Your son.

Whatever is of value and worth in his life
> has come by way of Your rich blessings.

His heart is glad in the realization
> of Your eternal presence.

He knows that he will never lose Your love.

I raise my voice in praise, O God,
> because no one can separate me from You.

Though circumstances threaten me
>> and my own obsessions entangle me,
> You will never let me go.

Your great power is sufficient to set me free
> from these things that hurt my soul.

If I put my trust in You,
> You will not allow them to destroy me.

I find so many reasons for praising You, O God.

O God, why have You left me?
Why are You so far from me?
I can no longer feel You near.
I reach desperately for You,
    but I cannot find You.

I know You are holy and all-righteous
    and everywhere present.
The saints of past years believed in You
    and trusted You.
You responded to their cries.
They sought for You, and they found You.
It is no wonder that Your praises
    were constantly on their lips.

But I feel as empty and insignificant
    as a bag full of wind.
I don't really expect men's plaudits,
    but I so sorely feel their criticism.
I risk all in following
      what I feel to be Your will for me;
      yet even my friends fail to support me,
      and they actually turn against me.
"He thinks he's doing God's will," they say.
"But he'll be sorry he made that decision."

I believe that You were with me
    from the very beginning of my life.

I know that You have cared for me
    through these many years.
But, God, I need You now.
I am in trouble,
    and I can't find You or feel You to be near.
O God,
    I feel in this moment as if I am falling apart.
Nothing seems to make sense anymore.
Everything I attempt to do ends in failure.
I feel inferior and weak.
Those I have tried to serve
    are actually gloating
        over my flops and failures.
I know, O God, that much of it
    is a matter of my foolish feelings.
The fact is, You are not far off.
You know both my feelings and my failings.
Yet You love me and accept me.
You will save me—even from myself.

Thus I will continue to sing Your praises.
In spite of or in scorn of my feelings
    I will celebrate Your loving presence.
As despicable as I may feel at times,
    You do not despise me, nor will You leave me.
Your love is personal, and it is eternal.

Nor will You despise or ignore the afflictions
    that plague Your many children.
Your sons and servants are precious to You.
Even when they fail You, You will never fail them.

You hear their cries and feel their pain
and are ever ready to support them
in their conflicts.

I dedicate myself anew to You, O Lord.
I will serve You
whatever the cost or the consequence.
You are my God.
Regardless of my feelings
of insignificance and inadequacy,
I will praise Your name and proclaim Your love
to men all about me.

23

The Lord is my constant companion.
There is no need that He cannot fulfill.
Whether His course for me points
        to the mountaintops of glorious ecstasy
        or to the valleys of human suffering,
    He is by my side,
    He is ever present with me.
He is close beside me
        when I tread the dark streets of danger,
        and even when I flirt with death itself,
    He will not leave me.
When the pain is severe,
    He is near to comfort.
When the burden is heavy,
    He is there to lean upon.
When depression darkens my soul,
    He touches me with eternal joy.
When I feel empty and alone,
    He fills the aching vacuum with His power.
My security is in His promise
        to be near to me always,
        and in the knowledge
        that He will never let me go.

24

Let us never forget that this world
    and everything in it belongs to God.
But not all of this world's citizens
    recognize or give allegiance to their Creator.

Who are they who truly love and serve God?
It is they who discover and live
    within His purposes for their lives.
It is they whose hearts and hands
    are dedicated to His will for them.
It is they who turn away from self-centered concerns
    to live for others about them.
They can count on God's perpetual blessings.
They nevermore need to be concerned
    about their personal salvation.
They have been delivered from such anxiety
    to focus their efforts on communicating
        God's eternal love to their fellowmen.

Let us look up and live!
God is present in all His glory and majesty.
Let us let go and celebrate!
Our loving Lord is here with us
    and will manifest Himself through us.
We are His vehicles and vessels.
We represent Him in all His saving power.
We are His beloved and empowered servants
    in this world that He created.

25

I am reaching for You again, O God.
From the abyss of defeat,
  the suffocating shame of failure,
    I seek Your mercy and Your help.
Enable me to see something of Your will for my life.
Break through this stifling darkness
  with some direction, some meaning,
  some purpose for my existence.
You are my God; You have promised me salvation.
How long must I wait for Your response?

Have You given me up, O Lord?
Are You remembering the uncountable times
  that I have failed You?
Then I am remembering Your steadfast love,
  that Your concern is for those
    who fail and fumble,
  that You seek to restore those
    who humbly reach out for You.

I know well that those
  who walk in Your course for their lives
    find contentment and fulfillment.
I have tried to do so, and again I have failed.
I am aware that those who serve You
  will know true security and abundance.
I have sought this only to be snared
  and incapacitated by my own weaknesses.

O God, have mercy!
I know my guilt is great.
Look upon my emptiness and loneliness,
 consider kindly my afflictions and despair,
 remember the perpetual presence
  of my human weaknesses and instincts.
Regard once more the pernicious and violent forces
 that oppose Your will in my life;
Forgive me my many sins,
 and restore me to Yourself.
Watch over me and hold on to me, O God,
 lest I fall again.

I am about to make an important decision, Lord,
    and the day before me is charged with uncertainty.
Enable me to sense Your presence,
    to feel Your undergirding power,
    to be assured of Your guiding concern.

I have been Your son and servant for many years.
Even in my youth I claimed Your redeeming love
    and dedicated my life to Your purposes.
Until now I have shunned the world's enticements,
    the human ambitions that so teasingly beckon,
    to pursue Your objectives
        and carry out Your commands.

I have been faithful to the hour of worship
    and the time of prayer.
I have celebrated Your grace and sung Your praises.
My dearest friends are those who love and serve You.

Now, O Lord, I have come to a fork in the road.
I don't know which way to turn.
I commit this day into Your hands.
I pray that it may be lived by Your direction
    and in accord with Your will.

I raise my voice in thanksgiving, O God,
    for You have granted me the assurance
        that You will guide my faltering steps.

27

With the living and eternal God as my goal and guide
    fear and anxiety preempt no place in my life.
All the evil in the world is not able to destroy Him,
    nor can it destroy anyone within His loving embrace.
The very legions of hell lay siege to my soul,
    only to be thwarted by a power far greater.

I have one primary and ultimate desire:
    to abide within the love and acceptance of God.
Within His tender care I know I am safe.

Thus I shall stand tall
    regardless of threatening enemies and the tyranny of evil.
I will counter the subtle voices of temptation
    with exclamations of praise to my God.

My God does hear when I cry out to Him.
He does not ignore my needs,
    nor is He indifferent to my desires.
He will not let me go
    even if my very own family should turn against me.
He will sustain me and keep me on course
    through the dangers and pitfalls of this life.

It is possible to know and experience God's love
    in this uncertain, tumultuous existence.
Take courage, step out in faith, scorning consequences.
Let God have His way with you.

O God, I am crying for help!
This is not a pious exclamation;
    I mean it! I'm desperate!
If You don't listen, I'll go down the drain!

Don't let me float downstream
    with those who ignore You.
I know they shall go over the edge if they persist
    in their course of rebelliousness and indifference.
Reach forth, O God,
    and snatch me out of this overpowering current
        lest I perish with them.

I thank You, O God.
You have heard my agonizing cry.
I called for You, and You responded.
You are my Hope and my Salvation.
I will sing Your praises forever.

And thus the Lord is the Hope and Salvation
    of all who trust in Him.
Stay close to those who struggle, O God;
    never let them go.

We need to give credit to whom credit is due.
God is alive,
 and He deserves our perpetual praises.
There is reason for rejoicing.
There is a God to worship and love.

His beauty is manifest
 in the skies and the forests.
His power is represented
 in the sweep of the ocean.
His majesty is portrayed
 in the gigantic bodies
  suspended in our universe.
The wind and the rain,
 the lightning and the thunder,
 the creatures that inhabit our land,
 the flowers that brighten our lives —
all this comes from God's hand.
The glory is not ours but God's.

Even the achievements
 of human hand, mind, and machine
 come by way of the wisdom and power
 of the eternal God.
The contributions of science,
 the fields ripe for harvest,
 the control of our rivers,
 the activity in our cities,

the establishment of our great institutions —
these also reflect the glory of God.

Let us give credit to whom credit is due.
Let us rejoice in the God who blesses us.
Let us seek His grace to serve Him
by serving others with the abundance
that He bestows upon us.

30

In a world where there are people
    who assume You no longer exist,
    I am compelled to proclaim Your praises, O God.
I cannot define or describe You,
    but I know by personal experience
      Your power and presence in my life.
There was a time when I screamed,
    "Good Lord, where are You?"
Then You touched my despairing soul with healing,
    and delivered me from my private little hell.
Thus I shout God's praises
    and exhort all who know Him to do the same.
There are times when I feel God's anger,
    but even then I know
      His concern and love for me remain eternal.
And my nights of despair
    resolve into the dawn of new joy.

There was a time when I thought I was secure
    amidst my material accumulations.
However, they gathered like a cloud
      to blot out the face of God,
    and I was left empty and unfulfilled.

I finally came to my senses
    and returned to You, O God.
"Lord," I said, "my well-deserved damnation
    would also be a loss to You.

I cannot praise You from the pits of hell
    or proclaim Your loving-kindness
        out of the grave of eternal death.
So have mercy, Lord,
    and help me out of this tangled web."

And You turned my griping into gratitude,
    my screams of despair into proclamations of joy.
Now I can explode with praises,
    and I will spend eternity in thanksgiving to You.

31

I am up a blind alley, Lord.
The props have been knocked out beneath me.
I feel as if I'm grappling with the wind
    for some support or security.
I've been pulled up short, Lord.
Now I realize how much I need
    something or someone, like You, Lord,
    beyond and above myself
        to give me stability to my tenuous existence.
Maybe it was Your doing, Lord.
It is Your way of bringing me back to home port,
    of correcting my focus
        and reassessing my goals.

I return to You with empty hands, Lord.
You know well my sorry plight.
I did not find that secret treasure,
    that pearl of great price.
The bright lights that beckoned
    only led me astray.
I became entangled in the bonds of self-service.
Everything I touched turned to dust in my hands.

I despise myself today, Lord.
Even those I thought my friends
    turn their faces from me.
There is no place to go, nothing to cling to.
I can only come back to You

and cast myself on Your loving mercy.
You are my God.
You have never let me out of Your sight.
Even when I strike out on my own,
    You pursue me and hold on to me.

I've stopped running, Lord.
From this point on
    I will dedicate my hours and days
       into Your loving hands.
I seek only Your guidance
    and the grace and strength
       to carry out Your purposes.
Restore me, O God, *to your designs*
    to Your program and design for my life.

Thank You for taking me back, Lord,
    for renewing my relationship with You.
I seek now to walk in Your course for me.
I shall abide forever in Your steadfast love.
I will proclaim Your praises
    and live out Your purposes.
Enable me to be faithful to You,
    whatever the consequences,
    and to celebrate Your love
       and communicate it to everyone around me.

The man who knows the meaning of forgiveness,
    whose past failures no longer plague him,
    who stands blameless and guilt-free before God —
    that man is rich indeed.

Every time I attempt to handle my own guilt —
    by ignoring it, rationalizing it,
    or just running away from it —
    some unseen power or pressure
      from the depths of my being
        squeezes my life dry, leaving me empty.

But when I face up to my failures and confess them,
    when I open my guilt-ridden heart
      to You, O God,
    then I realize the blessed meaning
      of forgiveness.

Thus everyone who claims faith in a loving God
    needs to cling to God's acceptance and concern.
Times of darkness will come,
    life's storms and tempests will continue to rage,
      but he shall not be destroyed by these things.

You are, O God, a place of refuge;
    You do enable me to face my problems,
    You do keep me from being destroyed by them.
Even within the darkness about us,

in the midst of life's turmoil,
one can often hear the voice of God:
"Even these things serve a purpose in your life.
Don't sell them short,
for they may be steps along My path for you.
Stop being stubborn and stupid
like some undiscerning jackass
that has to be driven with sticks or whips."

The faithful and the faithless both suffer
the uncertainties and insecurities of this life,
but the child of God can depend always
on the love of his Father.
It is for this reason that there is
light even in the midst of darkness
incomprehensible joy in the midst of sorrow,
and we can find
a measure of happiness and well-being
regardless of the circumstances that surround us.

33

God is here—let's celebrate!
With song and with dance,
  with stringed instruments and brass,
  with cymbals and drums,
 let us express ecstatic joy in God's presence.
Let us celebrate with the old songs of praise.
Let us also create new songs
  that portray the eternal love of our God.

He did create this world.
He continues to permeate it with His love.
Even among its frustrated and unbelieving children,
  He constantly carries out His purposes.
His plans for His world and its inhabitants
  are not obliterated by the foolishness of men.
His truth is not blotted out by the lethargy or lies
  of His apathetic creatures.
He continues to reign and to reveal Himself to us.

And God continues to create and to renew
  the world about us.
He does this through those who relate to Him,
  who rely on His ever-present love.
He delivers His children from the fear of death
  and through them gives life to this world.
God's love is sure and everlasting.
Hearts open to His love are filled with joy.
They truly find cause for celebration.

34

I feel at times as if I could never cease praising God.
Come and rejoice with me over His goodness!

I reached for Him out of my inner conflicts,
        and He was there
            to give me strength and courage.
I wept in utter frustration over my troubles,
        and He was near to help and support me.

What He has done for me He can do for you.
Turn to Him; He will not turn away from you.
His loving presence
        encompasses those who yield to Him.
He is with them
        in the midst of their troubles and conflicts.
He meets their emptiness with His abundance
        and shores up their weakness
            with His divine power.

Listen to me; I know whereof I speak.
I have learned through experience
        that this is the way to happiness.
God is ever alert to the cries of His children;
        He feels and bears with them
            their pains and problems.
He is very near to those who suffer
        and reaches out to help
            those who are battered down with despair.

Even the children of God must experience affliction,
   but they have a loving God
      who will keep them and watch over them.
The godless suffers in loneliness, without hope;
   the servant of God finds meaning and purpose
      even in the midst of his suffering and conflict.

35

It is not easy, Lord, to follow after You.
While You take the hard road
    with joyous leaps and bounds,
      I stumble over every stone
      and slip into every rut.
You calmly weather each storm
    and walk fearlessly through the night.
I am buffeted by the winds,
    and I falter in the darkness.

And You always have answers, Lord,
    for those who confront You.
My tongue is thick and clumsy.
I cannot articulate what I feel
    or what they need to hear.
You have the wisdom and the power
    to meet the needs of men about You.
But I am foolish and ineffective,
    and my brothers turn away from me in disgust.

I have really tried to relate to people about me,
    to reach out in love and concern.
I have shared their sorrows and their joys.
I have shelved my ambitions
    to respond to their needs.
But when I fail to produce what they want,
    or when I am limited by my humanity
      and incapacitated by my personal problems

they will have nothing to do with me.
I feel as if I have been used only to be abused.
I am squeezed dry and then cast aside
        as if I were of no further value.

Yet I must continue to follow You, O Lord.
It is a hard path to walk,
        and I will falter at times.
I long intensely for an occasional oasis
        along this journey through wind and sand.
I need desperately Your touch of joy and enrichment
        as I labor amidst the blood and tears
                of this distorted world.
I am empty, Lord,
        enable me to sense Your fullness
        and grant me the grace and the courage
                to be faithful as Your son and servant.

36

It amazes me how some can be utterly self-centered,
     so indifferent and calloused
        to the desires and needs of others.
Not only do they neglect God;
     they are totally oblivious of Him
        and have no fear of Him.
And then they convince themselves that this is life,
     that the world spins around them
        and they must satiate their own desires
           irrespective of the hurt it causes others.

And yet Your all-pervading love, O God,
     which extends far beyond
        the dimensions of our conscious lives,
     includes even these distorted people
        who spurn You in exchange for lives
           that are twisted and self-centered.

Your eternal love is beyond comprehension.
No wonder Your children reach incessantly for it
     and find security within it.
Within that love, O Lord, You answer our needs
     and the fulfillment of our desires.

Continue to pour out Your saving love
     upon those who follow You.
Allow not the arrogance and infidelity of the godless
     to deter me from Your course for my life.

37

It's high time we stop complaining
      about the dissipation of our world
         or the corruption of our society.
At the same time we eye with envy
      those ungodly characters
         who appear to have more fun
            or to be more successful than we are.

If we really trusted in God
         and were truly committed to His purposes,
         the world might be a great deal better off today.
God is in our world.
He is destined to be the source
      of our joy and well-being.
He is the fulfillment of our hearts' desires.
If we dedicate our lives to Him and His will,
      He will be able to work through us,
         to permeate this world's darkness
            with divine light.

Let's keep our cool and try to be patient.
Stop worrying
      about the apparent hopelessness of it all.
We only contribute to this despair
      by always being negative and defeatist.
God has not taken a vacation; He is here.
He has His own way of dealing
      with the instigators of corruption.

It will take time,
    but the victory is ultimately God's.
Those who live within God's will
    shall surely discover
      that His purposes prevail,
      that true joy and peace and security
        come from Him.

Let us wait on God and seek daily to obey Him.
He is our salvation and our security,
    and nothing in this world
      can take that away from us.
Let us calm our hositilities,
    overcome our anxieties,
      and walk in peace and love.

O God, how angry You must be with me!
I feel as if I were
    pierced through with a red-hot iron,
    stifled with the heavy hand of judgment.

I am falling apart.
I am sick unto death with sin and failure,
    broken and spent, wretched and miserable,
    flat on my face in despair.

Even those I once called my friends
        now keep their distance
    while others actually gloat over my predicament.
But I am becoming numb
    even to their glances of suspicion or pity
    and their self-righteous rebukes.
I have ceased trying to defend myself
    or responding to their accusations.
I've had it; I am ready to throw in the towel;
        I simply cannot take it any longer.

You are aware of my anguish.
You feel something of my misery.
I know that I have grieved You,
    and I am truly sorry for my sin.
Don't turn away from me, O God;
    don't leave me in this abominable mess.
Save me now, O God, lest I be damned forever.

39

I said to myself, "I'll watch it —
　　I'll grit my teeth and hold in my hostilities
　　　　at least as long as I
　　　　　　am in the midst of ungodly people."

And I honestly tried, but it was no use.
The pressures increased.
The more I stewed about it,
　　the more frustrated I became.

Finally I exploded:
"O God, demonstrate some concern for me.
Give me some reason for this incessant conflict,
　　some objective for this fast-ebbing life of mine.
You made me what I am — a bubble or a bag of gas,
　　and the span of my existence
　　　　is but a speck of dust to You.
It is true about every man.
He is no more than a smidgen of moist air
　　or a shadow without lasting substance.
Man enters and endures this temporal turmoil
　　for no reason whatsoever.
He agonizes and toils
　　only to leave the fruits for someone else to enjoy.

"So I wonder what in the world it's all about.
I have no hope at all except in You.
I continue to lay claim

to Your forgiveness for my failures.
Keep them from making me
    a despised and abhorred creature
        in the sight of men.
Lift Your heavy hand from me;
    I am utterly weary of its oppressing weight.
When You punish a man
      with judgment of his failures,
    You suck up like a tornado
      everything that is precious to him.
Surely man is no more than a passing cloud
    on the eternal horizon.

"Hear and decipher these confusing thoughts of mine;
    lend Your ear to these agonizing cries;
    turn not away from my pains and problems.
I am just a swiftly passing traveler
    as were all men before me.
Turn Your scornful eye away from me.
Let me have just a morsel of happiness
    before I leave this world
      and enter into oblivion."

Sisters of Christian Charity
Holy Family Convent and Infirmary
Danville, Pennsylvania 17821

40

I searched long and shouted loud for God.
It finally paid off, and He responded.
He reached into my pathetic emptiness
    and planted objective and purpose there.
Now I feel like singing;
    there is genuine meaning for my life.
And maybe I can sell others on this concept
    of really finding themselves in God.
Those who are thoroughly fed up
    with the fly-by-night objectives
      of this ephemeral existence,
    who will look to their Creator
      and seek out His will for them,
    they will also find something to sing about.
There is love and concern there,
    and meaning and purpose,
      far more than one can possibly imagine.

Our God is not looking for genius;
    He does not require great talents.
He is not charmed by our panic-ridden activity.
He simply asks for our faith and our obedience.
It was when I turned from self-seeking
    to embrace His will for my life
      that I discovered serenity and security.

Thus I am compelled to express in word and in deed
    the glad news of God's love and concern

to anyone who will listen.
And the Lord knows
that I have honestly tried to do this.
My frailties and my failures are many,
but I have not cheated on this score.
I have proclaimed the salvation
that God offers to all.

But my conflicts have not ceased.
My sin-permeated nature still plagues me.
I still feel overwhelmed at times
by my faults and fallibilities.
I am disturbed and depressed
when others fail to understand or accept me.
I need to rely continuously on the grace of God.

God grant that all who search for life's meaning
may discover such
in a relationship of love and trust in Him.
They shall then know His greatness
and proclaim His praises.
As for me, foolish and sinful though I am,
I know that God will never cease to love me.

41

I believe that he who gives of himself
    for the sake of others,
    who demonstrates genuine concern
      for those less fortunate,
    that he is especially blessed by God.
He is precious in God's eyes
    and is protected by Him.
Even as he faces the hatred of his enemies
    or the conflicts and illnesses of this existence,
    the Lord delivers and sustains him.

It is for this reason that I dare to claim
    God's gracious intervention on my behalf.
It is true that my sins are many.
I reach desperately for God's forgiving mercy.
I receive no comfort from many
    who I thought were my friends.
I could drop dead; they couldn't care less.
When we meet,
    their words are empty,
    their thoughts pregnant with suspicion.
When we part,
    they go out to spread their suspicions abroad,
      imagining the worst about me
      and whispering behind my back.

I can well imagine their conversation:
    "One would think he'd be

beyond this sort of thing;
and here he calls himself religious.
Why, he's as bad as the worst of them.
He's had it! He won't crawl out of this!"
Even the one person I trusted the most,
in whom I confided,
with whom I lovingly related,
even he looks down his nose at me
as one he would rather step on than support.
He no longer wants anything to do with me.

My loving God, You are truly gracious to me.
You have not cast me aside
or allowed me to be destroyed.
You know that I honestly want to serve You.
And You have demonstrated
Your acceptance and concern for me
in sustaining me
and drawing me even closer to Yourself.
May God be praised forever!

As a desert wanderer longs for springs of cool water,
    so my thirsty soul reaches out for You, O God.
How I long for a deeper sense of Your presence,
    for a faith that will embrace You
        without fear or doubt!
Yet while I weep in longing, people about me say,
    "If God is not dead, where is He?"

I remember so well the faith of my childhood.
How real God was to me in those days
    when I prayed and sang praises
        and listened to His Word
            in the fellowship of family and friends!
Then why am I so depressed now?
Why cannot I recapture the joy and confidence
    of those years?
I remember the stories of Your love
        that I had been taught;
        how merciful and all-powerful were Your dealings
        with Your children throughout history!
Yet now my heart is empty,
    and waves of doubt flood over my soul.

I pray, but the heavens, too, are empty.
It is almost as if God had forgotten all about me.
And while I struggle with the sickness of doubt,
    people about me say,
        "If God is not dead, where is He?"

O foolish heart, why do you seethe in unrest?
God has not changed;
 His love for me is ever the same.
I must renew my faith in God;
 I must again shout His praises
  even when I don't feel His presence.
For truly He is God,
 and He is my Help and my Hope.

43

O God,
    my life is cluttered up with conflicts.
And there are times
    when You seem so oblivious to it all.
The pitfalls before me, the weaknesses within me —
    all this is most depressing.
I feel as if I am groping in utter darkness.

Break into my darkness, O God.
Set me free from my hang-ups.
May these daily pressures
      that threaten to strangle me
    drive me to Your fountainhead of grace.
Then night will give way to the dawn,
    depression shall resolve into joy,
      and I shall sing Your praises once more.

O foolish spirit,
    why do you fret over so many things?
God is here!
He knows all about your troubles and trials.
Renew your faith in Him, and rejoice.

I shall rejoice!
No matter how black the night,
    God is my ever-present and eternal Hope.

O God,
 I have heard so much about how close You were
  to Your children throughout history.
They clobbered the enemy
 and credited You for their victories.
When they were defeated,
 they accepted their lot
  as Your righteous judgment.
They assumed they were Your beloved charges
 and even accepted their afflictions
  as from Your hand.
It was their persistent faith in You
 that held them together
  through the crises of their lives.

And I am aware of how You have watched over me
 in the midst of my conflicts.
You have enabled me to overcome
 many of the obstacles in my life.
Even when I so miserably failed,
 You set me on my feet again
  and directed me on Your course for my life.
I am keenly aware of my incapabilities,
 inadequacies, and of how much I need You.
I know all this, Lord.
You have been an integral part
 of my life's experiences.
I am deeply grateful for Your care and concern.

But what about now?
I am on the spot — and I can't reach You.
It seems as if You have left the scene
     and I am left holding the bag.
I cry for help
     and hear only the echo of my own voice.
I grope about me
     and find insurmountable walls and dark corners.
The advice of my peers and superiors
     seems devoid of genuine love or concern.
O God, if You are truly my God,
     reveal Yourself to me now.
I simply cannot bear the shame and the pain
     of my problem.
Nobody around me can help me.
If people knew about it,
     they would only shun me.

I have not forgotten You, O God.
I do believe in You as I have been taught.
I worshiped You and sang Your praises
     when all was well.
I have dedicated my life to You and Your purposes.
Now I am in deep trouble.
I have no one else to turn to.

O God, listen to me.
Respond to my cry for help.
Deliver me from this terrible conflict
     before it destroys me.
Help me to sense Your loving concern.
Save me before it is too late.

My heart is full of joy today.
I reach almost frantically for the sounds
      that might express that joy,
    the words that would proclaim the exuberance
      that I feel at this moment.
I am heavy with praise,
    and I must express it lest I succumb to it.

You, my dear friend, were the channel of this joy.
You touched me with love
    and awakened my sleeping heart
      to the beauty and fragrance of life about me.
God reached out through your devotion and concern
    to kindle anew a fire within me,
    to fan embers into flames of light and passion.
You marched into my jungle of despair
    and made a path for me to walk in once more.
You sliced through my confusion
    and gave order and motivation
      to my purposeless gropings.

I am so very grateful — to God and to you.
I pray that God may use me,
    as He has so abundantly used you,
    to transmit joy to the joyless,
      despairing lives of His children who cross my path.
And I pray that God may bless you
    and keep you and use you forever.

46

Our great God is still our Refuge and Strength;
    He is ever aware of our problems and fears.
Thus we have no business doubting Him,
    even though the earth is convulsed in tragedy
      or its human masses are threatened
        by nuclear annihilation.

God continues to reign as all-wise
    and as almighty as ever.
His eternal plan is not canceled out
    by the whims of men
      or the freakish accidents of nature.
Nations will destroy each other;
    civilizations will perish;
    the earth itself may one day become
    a smoking cinder, but God will not leave us.
He is forever our sure Refuge and Strength.

Just look about you; read the pages of history.
Refresh your flagging spirits with the reminder
    of His great feats throughout the ages.
And you will again hear Him speaking:
    "Relax, stop fretting, and
      remember that I am still Your God;
    I still hold the reins on this world of yours."

God is here among us;
    He continues to be our Refuge and Strength.

47

Clap your hands, stamp your feet!
Let your bodies and your voices
    explode with joy.
God is not some human concoction.
He is for real! And He is here!
Despite all attempts
     to rationalize Him out of existence,
   He is in our world,
     and He reigns over our universe.

The rulers of nations often ignore Him.
Men of learning often pass Him by.
The masses of His creatures substitute
    their own little gods in His place
   and worship the things they can see and feel.
There are others who build fortresses
    about themselves
   and manifest no need for God.

Our great God will not be ignored.
He will not remove Himself from our world.
Let us recognize His presence
    and fill the air with His praises.

How great is my God!
He soars above our poor intellects
    like a snow-capped mountain
       over a sun-baked desert.
He scatters the profound theories of wise men
    like leaves pushed around by a winter wind.
He shatters
    the assembled might of world governments
      as an earthquake levels a city.
He reaches down in tenderness
      to earth's poor creatures
    and draws them to Himself.

Consider with me the greatness of my God.
Measure His judgments;
    embrace His eternal love.
Stand tall in your faith
      courageous in your commitment,
    for He is truly a great God.

19

How foolish are the creatures of God!
They accumulate wealth
    and imagine themselves secure
        in possessions and property.
Or they utilize some inborn gift
    and dote on the plaudits of their peers.
They live for themselves alone
    and give no thought to eternity.
They claim that God is simply
    not necessary to their existence.
He is just a big thumb in the sky
    designed to pacify the weak and the childish.
They claim that man must be
    sufficient unto himself.
He doesn't need the extra baggage
    of faith or religion.

But when the riches melt away,
    health fails, talents wear thin,
        and remaining years become few,
    when no one honors them
    or expresses concern for them,
    then they stand naked and exposed
    in empty despair.
Their fortress is breached;
    they are flattened and defeated.
Life, what little of it there is left,
    no longer has meaning for them.

Then they may look desperately for the God
    whom they discarded in their youth.

Let us consider carefully the security
    of a loving relationship to God.
Let us mouth His praises
    and demonstrate in our lives the eternal joy
        of knowing and relating to Him.
We need not depend on this world's wealth
    nor the accolades of men.
We need not fear the end of our days
    upon this earth.
God is forever—
    and so the souls of those
        who are committed to Him.

Clap your hands, shout for joy!
God is real, and He is here!

God is indeed in our world.
From dawn to dusk,
    from twilight hours to the first light
        on eastern horizon,
    God is near us and around us.

God speaks to our world.
He speaks gently in love
    and thunders fiercely in judgment.
He calls to those who are faithful to Him.
He comforts them and challenges them.
He secures them and sends them forth.

God is at work in our world.
He works in and through the lives of His children
    who are loyal and obedient to Him.
"Don't bring your sacrifices to man-made altars
    or build shrines and erect memorials
        on My behalf,"
    He would say to us today.
"I already own the gifts you bring.
All these things have come to you from My hand.
You are to offer them on the altar of humanity's need.
These are the sacrifices that get through to Me
    and are accepted by Me."
It is thus that God touches the lives of needy men.
It is by way of the self-sacrificing love
    of His servants.

God judges our world.
This judgment falls upon those
        who live totally for themselves.
They are indifferent to the needs
        of their fellowmen.
No matter how impressive their rituals
            and religious exercises,
        their lives are not pleasing to God.

God is in our world.
We serve Him with the kind of worship
            and thanksgiving
        that effectively communicates His love
            to His children in need about us.

51

O God, may the measure of Your eternal love
    be the measure of Your mercy.
And may the measure of Your mercy
    be sufficient to blot out my great sins
        and cancel out the guilt of my wrongdoing.

I have failed, O Lord, and my failures
    weigh heavily upon my heart.
I cannot share them all with my brother
    lest they weigh too heavily upon him
        and may even threaten my relationship with him.
But You know what they are, O God,
    and how far I have fallen short
        of Your standards and expectations.

I am only human, Lord.
It was not by my choice that I was propelled
    into this fractured world.
The weaknesses that plague me
    are not all of my doing,
        nor can I handle them by my strength alone.

I know that nothing can be hidden from You.
I can only acknowledge my indictment
    and accept Your loving forgiveness.
Purge me of my guilt, O Lord;
    heal the hurts of those
        who have been afflicted by my failures.

Revive my flagging spirit, O God.
Restore to me the joy and assurance
    of a right relationship with You.
Reinstate me in Your purposes,
        and help me to avoid
            the snares and pitfalls along the way.

It is only then that my tongue will be set free
            to sing Your praises
        and my hands to perform the tasks
            You have set before me.
It is only then that I can relate
        deeply and meaningfully to my brother
        and communicate to him
            the message of reconciling love.

I bring You no oblation or sacrifice, my God,
        only a foolish and self-centered heart.
I do come to You with a sincere desire
        to be Your servant,
        to walk in Your course for my life,
        to receive Your love and channel it
            to my fellowmen about me.

I thank You, God, that this is acceptable to You
    and that I will remain Your son forever.

There are many clever people
       who apparently have no need for God.
With their keen wits and sharp tongues
       they seduce their fellowmen and use them
              to promote their own selfish ambitions.
They barge around in this world as if they owned it
       and have no consideration for those
              they hurt in the process.
They brashly step on one another
       in their avid pursuit of riches and power.
They scorn those they brush aside
       and destroy those who stand in their way.

They flaunt their achievements before men
       and brag about their self-sufficiency.
They demean those poor fools
       who support and applaud them
              in their ascent to their worldly thrones.

They will be toppled,
       these men and their thrones of clay.
From the dust they came;
       to the dust they shall return.
Their cleverness will dissolve into emptiness.
Their boasting will become like a hot wind.
Their achievements shall become as nothing,
       and they shall grovel before the victims
              of their atrocious acts.

This is not so with the child of God.
He may never know earthly success.
He may never be satiated with temporal riches.
But he is eternally secure in the love of His God.
Like a green tree that spreads its boughs
          to shield the weary traveler
       or holds out its fruit to the hungry stranger,
    he quietly and perpetually carries out
          God's purposes in a barren land.

Those who proclaim that God is dead
    are veritable fools.
They presume to speak
      as sophisticated intellectuals;
     they are in reality, even unconsciously,
      promoting depravity.

God is ever probing the hearts of men,
    marking those who are wise enough
      to seek after Him.

He finds instead
    that the great masses of His creatures
     are following after other gods.
And without realizing it,
    they are leading one another
      into certain destruction.
It is no wonder there is such confusion and terror
    in the world about us.
It is for most part perpetuated
    by those who have no use for God.
Oh, may our great God
    restore the hearts of men to Himself!

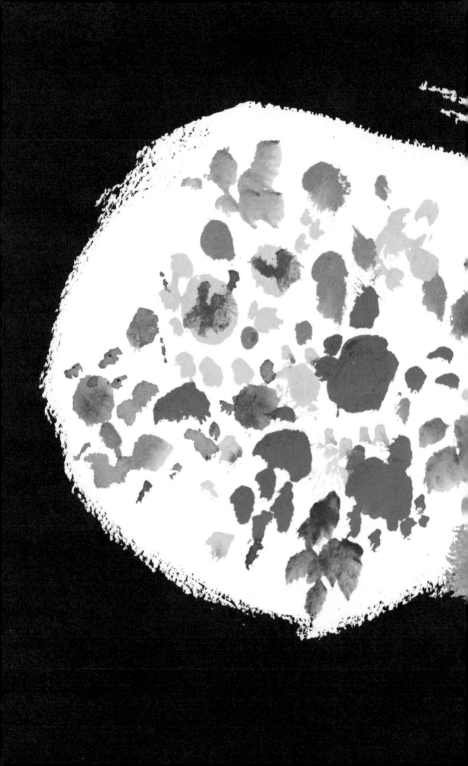

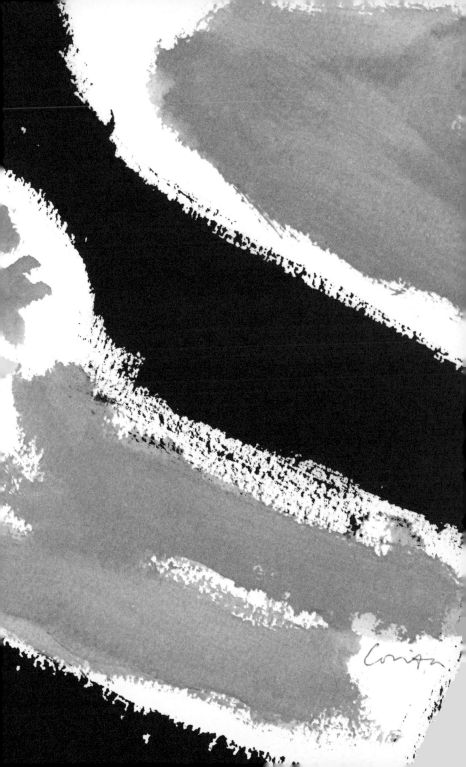

54

I come in thanksgiving and praise, O God.
Help me to articulate the gratitude
    that I feel toward You.

I was tripped up by my own pride
    and confounded by my foolishness.
I said things and did things that hurt others
    and dishonored You.
I stumbled into a net of my own making
    from which I could not escape.

Then You heard my cries and saw my plight.
You touched me with Your love and set me free
    to walk with You once more.
You continue to deliver me
    from the snares and pitfalls about me.

It is thus that I rejoice, O God.
It is because of this that I offer myself to You.
May Your ever-present love for me
    make me a vehicle of love toward others
      who are troubled and afraid today.

I am terribly alone, O God,
    and I don't know where to turn.
I thought I was really living
    when I came to the city —
    set free from the restraints
      of childhood and youth.
But now I am frightened.
The people around me are cold and indifferent.
No one knows that I exist.
The traffic by day and the neon glare
      that pushes back the night
    are strange and unfriendly.
I feel as if I am hopelessly lost
    in some concrete wilderness.
The streets lead nowhere —
    except to blend into other streets.
It's a wilderness filled with violence.
Its creatures are dazed, sick, hungry, or angry.
There is oppression and crime and injustice.
There is often blood in the streets.
People are being hurt here in the city.
And one can hardly see the blue sky by day
    or the stars by night
    or hear the song of birds
      or the tolling bells of a church.

It was exciting at first.
I even had a friend with whom to explore

the mysteries of the city.
Maybe I could have endured
    and found happiness with my friend.
But my friend turned into an enemy.
He no longer needed me
    and melted into the crowds
        that walk down my street.

Then the city became barren and desolate.
The bright lights became ghostly,
    the people about me like walking dead men
        or puppets on a string,
    the clamor and noise hideous and discordant.
And now my soul has become as bleak
    as the city about me.

I am lonely, O God, but I am not alone.
You are here in the city.
O God, help me to find You here in the city.
And enable me, my God,
    to serve You here in the city.

O God, I have tried incessantly
    to transmit Your love to people about me.
I shared my possessions;
    I gave of my time;
    I used Your gifts given to me to support,
        to help, and to bless others
            who were in need.

But I feel as if I had been used, O God.
People have wiped their feet on me.
They take what I offer and then go their way
    totally oblivious to my problems and pains.
They act as if I were in debt to them—
    as if it were my duty to share myself with them.

But even as I groan in complaint, O Lord,
    I know that this is Your course for me.
Even as they use You, so they will use me.
Truly, O God, I have nothing to lose,
    for it is in losing that I truly find
        that which is of everlasting value.

You are aware of my frustrations,
    my feelings of emptiness and loneliness.
You have promised to replenish my vessel,
    to make me a channel for Your eternal springs.
I am in debt, O Lord,
    to suffering humanity about me.

I must be emptied again and again—
    only to be filled from Your boundless resources
    and then to pour out once more
        Your blessings upon those who need.

You have delivered me from the wasteland of need.
Therefore I dedicate myself anew
    to the task of channeling Your gifts
        to the parched lives of others.

Encompass me with Your love and mercy,
gracious Lord;
I have no security except in You.
I am perpetually exposed
to the destructive forces of this existence.
I am in constant danger of losing the battle
to the very passions and desires
of my own nature.
I can only submit myself to You
and believe that You will fulfill
Your purposes in me.

Your love, O God, is steadfast;
Your grace is everlasting.

Even when I am beaten down by depression
and ensnared by my weaknesses and frailties
and my own lust threatens to devour me,
You are my God,
and You will not let me go.

I am determined to serve You, O Lord.
May my life be a continual thankoffering to You.
I shall sing Your praises forever.

58

My heart grieves, O Lord,
    over the leaders of this world
        who play god with the lives of men.
With the clever twisting of half-truths
    they gather followers into their folds
        and manipulate them
            into carrying out their purposes.
They blind men to personal conscience
        and responsibility
    and enslave them to the wishes
        and ambitions of the state.

Then there are starry-eyed mystics who assume
        they are God's special gift to mankind
    and who,
        through devious tricks or inscrutable gifts,
           create their little cults of loyal disciples.

You shall have the last word, O God,
    and those who take Your place,
        or who stand in Your way
           as You seek to draw men to Yourself,
        will be subjected to Your judgments.

You are my God, almighty and eternal.
Forbid, O God, that I should ever turn from You
    to follow the false shepherds of this world.

59

Deliver me, O God, from the enemies of my soul.
I am no longer afraid of men who stand in my way,
    even of those who obstruct Your purposes
    and who deceive their fellowmen
        with their arrogant and clever clichés.
They anger me, but they do not frighten me.
My pain and confusion come by way
    of my own weaknesses and faithlessness.

I strive for success and am fractured by failure.
I reach for ecstasy
    and am clobbered with depression.
I wait for guidance
    and Your heavens are gray with silence.
I ask for infilling
    and am confronted with emptiness.
I seek opportunities
    and run into stone walls.

I overcome these pernicious demons
        in the morning —
    only to face them again
        when day turns into night.
They refuse to die, these persistent devils.
They plague my days and haunt my nights
    and rob me of the peace and joy
        of God-motivated living.

And yet, O Lord, You have surrounded my life
     like a great fortress.
There is nothing that can touch me
     save by Your loving permission.
My faith will falter at times,
     but You will never fail me.
Teach me, O God, how
          to live by Your Word and promises,
          to sing Your praises,
          to carry on within Your purposes
               despite these taunting,
                    tempting enemies of my soul.

60

You made us, O God, a great nation.
The lands beyond our own
    tremble at our awesome might.
The rich wine of material wealth dulled our senses.
The tyranny of things obscured our vision.
We grew arrogant, self-satisfied,
    and were often insensitive to the needs
        of Your creatures beyond our borders.

We waved our swords menacingly
    at potential enemies of our great country.
We established our outposts
    in the very heart of the enemies' camps.
We extended our powerful tentacles
        into other nations' undeveloped resources
    and drew their blood into our own.
And we did this in Your name,
    and we convinced ourselves
        that it was by Your will.
Now our defenses have been broken down, O Lord.
Our fortress has been breached.
We have given birth to offspring
    that threaten us from within.
Oppressed people within our boundaries
    are rising up to assert their identity.
Our disillusioned youth are rebelling
    against our hypocrisy and insensitivity
        to human needs and rights.

Foreign philosophies are permeating
    our culture and our thinking.
Our self-centeredness has boomeranged
    and threatens to smother us in our own waste.
We are becoming paralyzed by fear
    and polarized by the extreme actions
        of radical and reactionary men.

Your Word is clear
    for those who would follow You, O God.
Your promises are assured
    for the nation that will worship You.
The enemies that threaten us
        and the problems that beset us
        can be absolved only in our returning to our God,
            and in allowing Him to guide us
                and through us to bless the world about us.
We seek Your help, O Lord,
    in restoring our great nation
        to those roots from which it came.

Listen to me, O God;
    listen to what I have to say.
From the bowels of this fractured world
    I cry out my fears and my longings.

I cannot find peace or security
    until I lose myself in something or someone
        that is greater than I.
Draw me more deeply into Your life and purposes;
    only then will I find shelter from the tempests
        of this fearful and uncertain existence.

You know that I am committed to You.
And as I am so committed,
    I have inherited the same divine promises
        that are given to all who follow You.
Grant to me the grace
    to fulfill my pledge of loyalty and service,
    and I shall never cease to sing Your praises.

As for me, my heart waits on God.
I know that my salvation comes from Him.
I may change my views about many things;
 but as for my need for God and His love,
  that is one conviction
   which shall never change.

There are many who would like
 to sabotage a man's deepest convictions.
With the skillful use of words and logic
 they try to destroy
  the very foundations of his faith.
As for me, my heart waits on God.
He is my Hope and my Help.
The temporal values that men focus on
 are so quickly lost
  amidst the tempests of this life.
Their highest aspirations
 burst forth like bright flares,
  only to fizzle out like wet fuses.

But my God offers a security that is eternal.
It cannot be logically defined,
 but it can be experienced.
Commit your life to Him,
 and you shall discover an anchor that will hold firm
 despite the chaos of this existence
  or the prattle of godless intellectuals.

Like a thirsty child reaching for a drink,
    I grasp for You, O God.
And I have found You.
I have sensed Your holy presence
      in the worship service;
    and in the hour of prayer
      I have felt You to be near.
I realize now that Your love for me
    is far better than life itself.

My heart is full of joy and contentment.
My mouth is filled with praises for You.
Even the night hours are no longer lonely
    as I contemplate Your tender concern for me.

The enemies of my soul still seek to betray me,
    but they shall not snatch me out of Your hand.
And now that I have found You,
    I shall be secure and happy forever.

64

Listen to me, O God;
    I think I have good reason to complain.

I try very hard to follow in Your paths
    and to serve in Your purposes.
But I am so deeply disturbed
    over the enemies and pitfalls
      that I unsuspectingly meet
        around every corner.
I find them in the tumultuous passions
    of my own being.
Much as I seek
    to rid myself of these overwhelming forces,
    they continue to clutch at my soul
      and to trip me up as I strive to please You.
I become so tired of this perpetual conflict
    with my sin-permeated nature.

And then I run into the opposition
    in the reactions of well-trusted friends.
Their suspicions and unjust criticisms
    leave me withered and dried up
      in depression and discouragement.

And now it is the cunning words of the worldly-wise,
    even the intellectual giants of this age,
    that threaten the very foundations
      of what I so intensely believed in.

I must renew my faith and continue to believe
     that those who foolishly oppose You
        will fail in their attempts
           to thwart Your purposes
     and that those who trust in You
        are truly and eternally secure
           even in the midst of this conflict and antagonism
           that swirls incessantly about them.

You well deserve the praises of men, O God;
    and they should fulfill their pledges to You.

Everyone must eventually face up to You,
    and it must be with all
        of his sins and shortcomings.
But anyone who comes in sorrow and repentance
    shall find You merciful and gracious.
You shall forgive his sins,
    and You shall reconcile him to Your kingdom
        and fill his heart with Your love and joy.

O God, You reach out to save us,
    You are the single, eternal Hope of all mankind.

You make Your power known to us
    in the majestic grandeur of the mountains,
    in the thunderous roar of ocean waves.
Your abundance is poured out upon us
    in the grain-laden fields,
        the flocks in the meadows,
            the gentle rain that caresses the green hills.
Your love for us is manifested
    in Your great acts of deliverance on our behalf.

You well deserve the praises of men, O God.

It is high time we start making
   happy noises about God,
   that we boldly proclaim His name
   and shout His praises.

We already know
   what He has done throughout history,
      the great deeds He performed,
      the people who witnessed them
         and worshiped Him.
Let us recognize, as well,
   what He is constantly doing for us.

He draws us into the crucible of conflict;
   He tests and tries us
      in the valley of pain and sorrow;
   He allows us to taste the agony of affliction;
   He gives our enemies permission
      to oppose and oppress us.
And then He uses these very things
   to purge and prepare us for His purposes.

Now I renew my pledge to my God.
I strive to carry out those promises I made to Him
   when I cried for His help in my troubles.
I yield up to Him my life
   as a sacrifice and thankoffering.

You who are seeking for God,
    these are the things He has done for me:
He has accepted me despite my sins and failures.
He listens when I cry out to Him,
    and He responds with solace and support.

I proclaim God's praises
    because I know He will love me forever.

May we continually be
    the recipients of God's mercy and blessing
  in order that we may demonstrate
    His order and purpose throughout the earth
    and His redemptive power
      to the creatures of this world.

And may it ultimately resolve
  in all of God's sons lifting their voices
    in praise to their Lord and God.

The nations of the earth would truly
    abide in peace and sing for joy
  if they would allow God to be their God
  and if they would direct their destinies
    according to His will.
Then the inhabitants of this world would surely
  lift their voices in praise to their Lord and God.

The earth continues to receive
  the abundance of God.
His blessings are all about us.

May every mountain and valley, plain and forest,
    every city with its teeming apartments,
  and every sprawling suburb
    echo with the praises of men to their God.

We long for when God will take over our cities,
    when wickedness shall be suppressed
        and selfishness subdued,
    when people will begin to care for one another.

There will be clean air to breathe
    and pure water to drink.
There will be better schools for the young,
    hospitals for all who are ill,
    and jobs for those who seek them.
Everyone will feel needed and loved in such a city:
    the child, the laborer,
    the executive, the senior citizen.
There will be dignity and freedom and equal rights,
    whatever one's ethnic or economic backgrounds.
There will be homes to live in
    and parks to play in.
There will be libraries and theaters
    and halls of learning.
There will be a place for everyone to live
    and work and learn and rest and play.
And people will have time for one another.

O how we will praise God in such a city!
Our voices will join in a great chorus of celebration.
We will daily offer up thanksgiving to our God,
    who rules over our city.
And everyone will have time for one another.

But God does not rule over our cities.
Our streets are pregnant with crime.
The poor and dispossessed pack into ghettos.
Our schools are overcrowded and inadequate.
We choke on the air we breathe.
We stumble over our own litter and waste.
We neglect the old and ignore the young.
We rush pell-mell from pillar to post.
And no one cares for one another.

You seek, O God, to rule over our cities.
You have given us pure air and green hills
    and great forests and clean rivers.
You have showered upon us Your abundant gifts —
    all that we need to make our cities splendid.
And You have given to us Your love
    and the responsibility to care for one another.

This has been our great failing, O God:
    we have sucked to our individual bosoms
        the gifts of Your love,
    but we have never really learned
        how to care for one another.

You have rebuked us for our selfishness, O Lord.
We are smothering in the waste
    of our self-centered living.
Deliver us, O God,
    restore to us those cities in which You dwell,
    and teach us, our loving God,
        how to care for one another.

69

O God, at this time I find myself
  really up against the wall,
    at the bottom of the barrel,
    at the end of my rope.
There is no place to go but up.
Save me, O God, before it is too late.

I can't even cry out any longer;
  I can't even pray, so deep is my despair.

O Lord, You know the ugliness of my failure.
How sorely it must grieve You!
Forbid that others may be hurt by my foolishness,
  that my errors and faults might lead them astray.
I have been trying to represent You before them;
  instead I have brought dishonor and disrespect
    on my witness and Your name.
Now even those who once loved me
    keep their distance;
  and those who listened in respect
    turn away in disgust.

Maybe it has been
      my intense eagerness to carry out Your purposes
        that has become my stumbling block,
    and now I am being ridiculed for my zeal.
They make fun of me;
    they whisper about me behind my back.

O God, don't let me go down the drain.
Respond, in Your great love,
    to my unhappy plight.
Raise me from the mire of despair,
    the darkness of depression.
Deliver me from these human weaknesses
    that beset me and lead me into defeat.
You know what they are, O Lord,
    and You know the limits of my endurance.
You know, as well, the pain of my failure
    and the abject loneliness one feels
        when he loses the battle.

You know, O God,
    and You reach forth in mercy
        to rescue and deliver.
You sometimes permit failure
      and defeat in my life,
    only to revive and renew
        my relationship to You.
Thus I will again sing the praises of God
    and make thankofferings to Him.

May all those who are
      beaten down by failure and despair
    see anew Your love
    and experience Your deliverance
    and be restored once more
      to joy and purposefulness.

O God, may You take pleasure in setting me free
        and in securing me
            from the enemies of my soul.
Keep them from bringing
        shame upon Your servant
        and dishonor upon Your name.

May those who sincerely seek You
            find genuine happiness and fulfillment,
        and may they express their joy
            in proclamations of praise to God.
As for me, I am always
        in need of Your sustaining grace.
O God, do not withhold it from me.

71

Good Lord, You have kept me
within the secure embrace of Your love
these many years.
My life is one long list of divine deliverances.
I have come running to You again and again
when the forces of evil
set themselves against me.

From the moment of my birth
I was dedicated to Your will,
given life by You,
only to yield it back to You.
And since that time the days and hours of my life
have been filled with praise for You.

But the enemies that plagued me in my youth
still lay siege to my soul,
looking for chinks in my armor,
for loopholes in my defenses
through which to enter and lay waste.

Now, as I near
the late afternoon and evening of my life,
I continue to seek out Your love and mercy.
Even while I shout Your praises
and proclaim Your salvation,
I reach for the assurance
of Your love and concern.

You have guided me
    through my precarious youth,
    now I need Your grace for my senior years.
Fill my heart with purpose
    and my mouth with praises
    that I may continue to proclaim
        Your name and Your salvation
        to all who will listen.

You are, O God, the Creator and Performer
    of great and glorious things.
There is no one like You.
You have kept me amidst life's conflicts,
    led me through its crucible of experiences,
    drawn me back from its pitfalls and precipices,
    healed all my wounds
        and comforted me in my afflictions.
Thus I know that You
    will continue to love and care for me.

I will dedicate my remaining days
    to praising You,
        espousing Your faithfulness
        and proclaiming Your love and concern
            for all who will turn to You.
May every fiber of my being and
    every activity of my life
        resound with praises to my God.

72

O God of love,
>> grant to Your sons and servants the grace
>> to represent you effectively
>> in our discordant world.
Give us the courage
>> to put our lives on the line
> in communicating life and truth
>> to all Your creatures
>> wherever they may be found.
Where there is injustice,
> may we diagnose its cause
> and discover its cure.
Where there is bigotry,
> teach us how to love
> and how to encourage others to love.
Where there is poverty,
> help us to share the wealth
> that has come from Your hand.
Where there is war and violence,
> may we be peacemakers that lead men
>> to Your eternal peace.

Help us, O God, to become what You
> have destined and empowered us to become.
Where there is darkness,
> may we become the rays of Your sun
> that banish the gloom of lonely lives.
Where there is drought,

let us be like fresh showers
    that turn barren deserts into green meadows.
Where there is ugliness and distortion,
    enable us to portray the beauty and order
      of Your will and purposes.

Great God, You are in our world.
Your majesty is reflected
    in Your creation about us.
But there are multitudes who do not
    feel Your concern or
    acknowledge Your love.
Is it because Your servants have failed
    to carry out Your command and commission
    that we have yet to sense
      the significance of our salvation
      and the purpose of our mission?

Forbid, O God,
    that we be deaf to the cries of the poor
    and indifferent to those who have needs.
May we identify with those who are oppressed
    and help to bear the burdens
    of those who suffer about us.
May we hear Your voice of concern
    and feel Your loving touch
      through Your servants who are in this world
      to manifest You to men about them.
The glory is Yours, O God,
    and we shall praise Your name
    and celebrate Your cause together.

13

It is generally expected
     that God will stand by the righteous
     and relate to those whose deeds and thoughts
          are purely altruistic.
I am afraid I just don't belong
     to that class of people.
I guess I am just a perpetual backslider.
Rather than thinking unselfishly,
     I find myself envious and covetous
          about those who have so much more than I.

They never seem to have problems.
They are always so strong and healthy.
I doubt that they know the meaning of conflict.
They are proud, carefree,
     devil-may-care, even malicious,
          and so disgustingly smug about it all.
They act as if God didn't even exist,
     and they are almost blasphemous
          in their attitudes and actions.

And yet people will honor and applaud them;
     they find nothing to censor about them.
What aggravates me is their obvious unconcern
     about God or fellowman.
Yet they always appear to be
     so comfortable and well off.
And all the while I struggle so desperately

with my sin-permeated nature.
I try so hard to please God,
　　yet my days are full of conflict
　　　　and my heart seethes in unrest.

I know I speak foolishly and unfairly,
　　but I get so fed up with it all.
That is, until I begin arguing with God about it.
Then I realize that they are
　　not as well off as they appear to be.
Their bright bubble will burst one day;
　　their dream will turn into a nightmare.

It's just that I get so depressed at times,
　　and I act like a stupid fool.
What is so amazing
　　is that even while engrossed
　　　　in irrational and unspiritual contemplations
　　I am never far from You.
You hold me close to Yourself.
You guide me and watch over me.
You assure me that it is all worth it.
And because of this glorious truth
　　I really have no need for anything else.
The essential desires of my being are met in You.
I shall often be victimized by human failure,
　　but my great God never ceases
　　　　to love me and bless me.

How good it is to know that God is always near!

74

It is disturbing and discouraging, O God,
        to witness the apparent successes
            of those who oppose You.
While Your children wrestle
        with doubts and conflicts,
        the agnostics of our world
            are tearing down the pillars of our faith
            and gloating over our frustration.

They have made fun of our rituals and symbols.
They are dissecting our dogmas
        and ridiculing our institutions.
They create godless philosophies
        that seduce the young and confuse the old.

They deliberately obstruct our efforts
        to represent You in our world.
As a result of their diabolic activities,
        many are turning away from the true God
            to worship lesser gods
            and to expend their lives on lesser goals.

We know, O God, how You have handled
        Your enemies in the past.
We know that You cannot be dethroned,
        that You are God over all creation.
Then how can You allow these god-defiers
        to get by with what they are doing to us today?

Consider our restlessness, O God.
Do not let us be stepped on and ground under.
Help us, O God,

  ineffective and foolish as we may be,
 to stand up to the demigods
  that plague our land.

75 and 76

We praise You, O God.
Even in the midst of this world's wickedness
    we celebrate Your majesty and power.

For You are here, O God.
You are here to save;
    You are here also to judge.
Even while the godless trumpet their rebellion,
    You hold the world in the palm of Your hand.
Should You close Your hand in anger, O God,
    their doom is sealed,
    their boasts ended forever.

Your fainthearted servants
    need not be dismayed, O God.
Even the rebelliousness of Your obstinate creatures
    can serve to further Your purposes.
We need not fear the distortions
    of those who defy and oppose You.
We need only renew our relationship to You,
    rededicate our lives to Your objectives,
    and continue to celebrate Your presence
    and Your power in our world.

77

I cry to God in my desperation.
Out of the dark corner of my stifling loneliness
    I grope in vain for some solace or comfort.

I try to think about God,
    to contemplate His many promises;
        but my heart is empty,
            my soul as dry as dust.
I spend sleepless nights searching,
    waiting for God to speak to my need,
        to give me strength in my conflict.
I remember how He has responded
    to my prayers in times past,
    but I get nothing from Him now —
        nothing save the echoes of my own agonies
        screamed into empty heavens.

I am reminded of His deeds
    and wonders of years past.
He demonstrated His love
    in His concern for His people.
His majesty and power are reflected
    in the great forces of nature about me.
Then why doesn't He hear my pitiful pleadings?
Why doesn't He fulfill His promises on my behalf?
Good Lord, where are You?

It would be good for us to consider God's dealings
    with men and nations throughout history.
We ought to know these things;
  - we have heard them again and again.
But we forget so quickly,
        and we fall so foolishly into the same pitfalls
            of infidelity and purposelessness.

God reached down and gathered a people for Himself.
He drew them into His fortress of love.
He revealed Himself to them
        through His commandments
            that taught them how to live together in peace.
He enabled them to sense His presence
        in miraculous ways.
He poured out upon them
        all that was needed to sustain them.
Even in the barren desert
        food was rained upon them from heaven
        and water burst forth
            out of the very rocks around them.
He sent them prophets to teach them
        and warriors to guide them
            through enemy country.
Like a shepherd who watches over his flock,
        our Lord watched over His children.

But like silly, confused sheep,

the children of God went astray.
They became self-sufficient and wandered off
    to pursue their own selfish interests.
Many of them rebelled against their God.
And God, in His love, had to let them go
    because they refused to accept His love
        and to walk in His paths before them.

They became lost in the desert.
They suffered sorely for their sins.
They were hungry and thirsty and afraid.
Only then did they remember
    the Creator of their youth
    and the loving care of their heavenly Father
        in those days when they walked in His paths.

Some of them turned back to God again.
They discovered once more their loving God,
    a God willing to forgive them and accept them,
        to gather them once more
            into His fortress of love—
        to care for them and watch over them
            like a shepherd over his flock.

Like silly, selfish sheep,
    we often wander off on our own,
        imagining that we can find
            our own way to joy and security.
We discover pain
    and emptiness
    and meaninglessness
        outside the orbit of God.

We are out of joint,
    and the deepest longings of our hearts
        go unfulfilled.

I return, O God, to You
    and Your purposes for my life.
I find You waiting for me,
    ready to forgive my foolishness
      and my rebelliousness
    and eager to reinstate me in Your family
      and reconcile me to Your will once more.

I thank You, O God,
    for drawing me back to Your loving heart.

79

Why is it, O Lord,
> that the ungodly appear to be so successful?
They have no use for the church.
They play fast and loose with the lives of others.
They live solely for themselves
> and have no concern for others
>> except to use them
>>> to further their personal ambitions.
They not only obstruct Your purposes, God,
> they pollute Your world and taunt Your servants.

Why do You let them do it, O Lord?
Why don't You avenge Your enemies?
Why don't You show them
> through Your faithful servants
> that we are on the right course,
> that success comes to those
>> who love and follow You?

Help me, O God, to love Your enemies
> even as You love them,
> to bear patiently and graciously their scorn
> and to serve You faithfully
>> whatever the consequences.
Help me to measure my worth and success
> by Your standards
> and to rejoice in Your love and acceptance.

O God, You are the Creator
and the Sustainer of Your church.
You have protected and prospered
Your faithful followers
throughout the stormy and tumultuous past.

Today we are in trouble.
Listen to our cries of consternation, O God.
We are confused and confounded.
We don't know where to turn,
in what direction to go.

We have prayed, O God.
We have sung Your praises.
We have proclaimed Your love to the world.
But today our power is slipping away,
our prestige is wearing thin.
People seem to have little respect for us anymore.
Those who have been brought up
within our structures
and have embraced our doctrines
are leaving the fold.
They say we are no longer meeting their needs
or the needs of the world.

You were with us in the beginning, Lord.
You planted us in the midst
of this world's turmoil.

127

You nurtured us and watched over us.
In spite of Your enemies,
   who sought to destroy us,
   we grew until we encircled the earth.
Great shrines were built in Your honor, Lord.
Magnificent institutions were established
   to carry out Your purposes.
Men dedicated their many skills
   to perpetuate Your teachings.
Multitudes gathered to declare Your praises.

Today we are in trouble, Lord.
The walls are crumbling.
Our sanctuaries no longer attract the masses.
Men's skills are dedicated to other purposes.
We no longer are making much of an impression
   on this world of ours.

Renew Your church, O God.
We know You will never turn away
      those who come to You
   and will forever sustain
      those who trust in You.
Fan the dying embers, Lord.
Stir us up, and restore us to the position
   of power and effectiveness.
Give us new life and new vision
   that we may advance Your kingdom
      in our disjointed world.
Renew Your church, O God,
      and revive Your servants,
   so that the whole earth may know of Your love.

81 and 82

Our great God has heard our cry,
  and He is speaking to His church today.
I hear Him saying many things.
He reminds us that He is God in our world,
    the God who piloted His people through history,
      who regards His church with love and concern.
He would have us remember
    how He freed us from sin's burden and guilt,
    how He responded to our pleas for deliverance
      and was present with us
        in the trials and conflicts of our lives.
He brings to our remembrance the many times
      we neglected to listen to Him
    and how He had to allow us to hurt ourselves
      because we stubbornly chose our own course.
He reiterates His promise to meet our needs
    and to enrich our lives
      as we rely on Him for grace and strength.
He diagnoses our sickness even today
    and points us to His purpose for our existence.

We have become complacent
    in our structures and institutions.
We have been subtly diverted
    from His will and purposes in our world.
We have selfishly interpreted His Word
    to fit our schemes and carry out our intents.
We have clutched at God to pacify and sustain us

even while we remain insensitive
to the suffering world about us.

Now God is speaking again,
in judgment as well as with promise.
He is reaching out to restore us to Himself
and to renew our vision for His world.
"How long will you ignore
My oppressed and dispossessed children,
their cries for liberty and justice?"
our God is saying to the church.
"Why are there people going hungry about you
while you abound in gifts from My hand?
You are My sons and servants,
My representatives in a fractured world.
I can reach those sick, needy, loveless,
and lonely creatures only through you.
This is the reason I have given you so much,
that you may share it with them."

Help us, O God,
to return to Your purposes for Your church,
to recognize all men as Your subjects,
that the world belongs to You.
May Your great love flood our lives
only to overflow and touch with healing
and to channel Your grace to the lives
of every one of Your children.

You are in our world, O God.
May we serve You here by ministering
to the needs of our fellowmen.

I am so depressed tonight, O God.
I feel as if I am the sole target
    of an enemy barrage —
    that all the demons of hell are bent
        upon damning my soul for eternity.

I remember Your precious promises,
    but I do not witness their fulfillment.
I talk to people about Your love,
    and they drown my zeal with scorn.
I step forth to carry out Your will,
    but I feel no sense of accomplishment.
I mouth words, wave my arms,
    and beat the air with fruitless endeavor.
Then I fall like a wounded warrior,
    bone-weary, defeated, and lonely.
And I wonder if You are truly my God,
    and if I am really Your child.

Consume, O God, these demons that depress,
    these enemies that plague my soul.
May the whirlwind of Your Spirit
    sweep them out of my life forever.
May I awaken with a heart full of joy,
    and with the strength and the courage
        to walk straight and secure
            in the dangerous
            and difficult paths before me.

O God, the center of Your will
    is truly the place of fulfillment.
I long incessantly
    for the peace and security of walking with You.
Therein only is purpose and meaning for my life.

Even the birds of the air
      and the animals that inhabit our forests
      abide within Your orbit and destiny for them.
Thus it is that the man
      who discovers and follows Your course for him
      is forever blessed.

How enriched they are
    who draw their power from You,
    whose hearts are focused on You!
Even as they wend their way
      through this fractured world,
    they become springs of healing,
      reservoirs of power,
        to the sick, weak, and empty lives
        they touch about them.

O Lord, look with loving mercy upon those
    who have yielded their destinies to You.
Just one day in the center of Your will
    is incomparably better than a thousand
      spent in the pursuit

of self-centered aims and objectives.
It is more fulfilling to be an underpaid clerk
in the service of my God
than to be owner and director
of some huge and wealthy enterprise.

O God, nothing that is
truly good and worthwhile
is withheld from those who walk
within Your will.
The man who trusts in You is very rich indeed.

O God, You have indeed been good to us.
You have prospered our land.
You have opened Your heart to us in love.
You have forgiven our sins
    and adopted us as Your sons.

But now our country is in turmoil.
We no longer have confidence in our leaders.
Our citizens are in revolt.
Our young men are spilling their blood
    in foreign wars.
People are turning away from You
    and are being ensnared
        by strange doctrines
        and godless philosophies.

We know that You have not turned away from us.
You touch with joy and peace
    the hearts that are open to You.
You stand ready to show Your salvation.
    to all who will trust in You.
As we speak to You in faith,
    You respond in loving concern.
You will give us what is good
    and will prosper us
        with gifts from Your hand.
You are holy and just.
You love Your children

and will guide them
   in Your course for their lives.

Renew our faith, O God.
Forgive us our many failures and infidelities.
May our land continue to be a place
   where we can be free to love and serve You.

O Lord, my prayer to You is always
    out of a life that is full of need.
I am Your servant; child
    I am trying to represent You.
I need Your support for every step I take.
How gracious You are to hear my plea
    and respond to my cry
    and pour out Your forgiving love upon me!

Men are so foolish
    in the things they love and worship.
You alone are God,
    and You alone possess the healing grace
        that can succor and sustain their fickle hearts.
Continue to lead me in Your course for my life.
Enable me to walk in the way of truth.
Draw together in loving obedience to You
    all the members and senses
        of my body and being.
Then I shall glorify You forever,
    and my life shall be
        a perpetual thankoffering to You.

I find the daily journey
    not only difficult but painful.
There are forces within me and about me
    that are much too strong for me.
But You are a loving and patient God.

Continue to have mercy upon me,
　　　to stir me from the doldrums of sin,
　　　to deliver me from my selfish involvements,
　　　to forgive me my sins and failures,
　　　to shore up the weak places in my life.
Help me
　　　to feel something of Your loving acceptance
　　　and to reflect to others
　　　　the joy of being Your son and servant.

This world is God's world.
And our great God loves the world that He made
    and the beings He created to people it.

The black people, the brown people,
    the yellow and the white,
    those with slant eyes or straight noses,
    the rich and the poor, lowly or noble —
they are all God's people,
    and His love embraces each and every one.

Not all the creatures of this world
    are citizens of the kingdom of God.
The people who shun His redeeming love
    cannot inhabit the city of eternal light.
They become the children of darkness.
They shall wander forever
    through the limitless spaces of nothingness.

The sons and daughters of God are those
    who relate to their Father and Creator,
    who walk in obedience to His will and Word.
They shall dwell together in joy
    and shall sing and dance
      in perpetual celebration
      in that beautiful city
        beyond the boundaries and borders
        of this present world.

O God, I need You every day that I exist
    and every night that I pass through.
Never turn Your face from me, O Lord,
    for my life is a perpetual plea for help.

My life is one long series of conflicts and defeats,
    and they only increase as I near its end.
My ultimate destiny is a hole in the ground,
    but even now I am as good as dead.
Without strength, forsaken,
        shunned by my fellowmen,
    I feel as if I were separated forever from You.
I am assailed by afflictions,
        beset by obsessions,
            and all but forgotten by God and man.

And yet I continue to cry out to You.
Even while the assaults of this life
            and the fear of death
        surround me and close in on me,
    I look to You for some ray of hope.

Good Lord, where are You?
Is there nothing within me worth saving?

I feel like singing this morning, O Lord.
I feel like telling everyone about me
        how great You are.
If only they could know the depths of Your love
        and Your eternal concern for those
                who will follow You!
But my songs are so often off-key.
My speech is so inadequate.
I simply cannot express what I feel,
        what I know to be true about Your love
                for Your creatures upon this world.

But even the songs of the birds
        proclaim Your praises.
The heavens and the earth beneath them,
                the trees that reach toward You,
                the flowers that glow in colorful beauty,
                the green hills and soaring mountains,
                the valleys and the plains,
                the lakes and the rivers,
                the great oceans that pound our shores —
        they proclaim Your greatness, O God,
                and Your love for the sons of men.

How glorious it is to be alive, O Lord!
May every breath of my body,
        every beat of my heart,
                be dedicated to Your praise and glory.

90

O God, You have always been God.
Long before the earth was formed,
        long after it ceases to exist,
        You have been and You shall always be.

With You there is no beginning or end;
        time is not measured by decades or centuries.
Our precious lives, so important to us,
        are but fleeting shadows to You.
And they are so full of trouble and conflict
        and so marked by sin and failure.

O God, break into our short span of existence
        with Your eternal love and grace.
May our days of despair
        be interspersed with hours of joy.
Enable us
        to see something of Your will and purpose
            for our creation
        and to discover some meaning
            for our brief and trouble-fraught
                appearance in this world.
Imprint upon us Your brand of ownership,
        and place us
            within Your plan and objective for our lives.

91

That one whose faith is focused on God,
    who finds his security in Him,
    does not have to live in fear.
He is not left untouched
    by the tempests of this life,
    and he may be wounded
    by the onslaughts of evil,
But his great God does not leave him
    to suffer these things alone.
The Lord cares for His own and delivers him
    even in the midst of the conflicts
    that plague him.

If God is truly your God,
    you do not have to be afraid
    of the enemy that threatens
    or the affliction that lays you low.
Men all about you may fall,
    never to rise again,
    but the Lord is by your side
    to raise you to your feet
    and to lead you to ultimate victory.

Even the ministering spirits of His invisible world
    are watching over you.
They will not allow anything to hurt you
    except by God's loving permission
    and through His eternal concern.

Our loving God has promised it:
"Because My child loves Me,
        I will never let him go.
I shall feel the pain of his wounds
            and bear his hurt
        and shall transform that which is ugly
            into that which enriches and blesses.
And when he cries out in agony,
        I shall hear and answer him.
I will be close to him and will deliver him,
        and I will grant him eternal life."

92

It's a glorious feeling to be able
    to unload my heart,
    to spill out my gratitude
        in thanks to You, O God.
Morning, noon, and night
    I want the whole world to know of Your love.
I want to shout it, to sing it,
    in every possible way
        to proclaim Your praises,
        to express my joy.

How great You are, O Lord!
Your thoughts are unfathomable,
    Your ways beyond comprehension.
And all the while we are still confounded
    over the problem of evil.
We simply cannot understand
    why the ungodly appear to be so successful,
    why good fortune seems to follow those
        who defy You.
But we know their success is short lived.
Those who refuse to turn to You will never find
    that ultimate and total fulfillment
        that is promised to the sons of God.

The children of God,
    those who open their lives to You,
    portray the wonder and beauty of Your Spirit.

They are like springs of water in a parched world.
They flourish even amid the distortions
    and the ugliness around them.
Their lives are rich and productive
    in a barren and desolate society.

Help us, those of us who love You, O God,
    to prove to our disjointed world
        that You are in our midst.

It may not always be apparent,
    but God does reign over our world.
He rules in majesty and might,
    and no philosophy or power
        can cast Him from His throne.

He allows us to cross up His purposes —
    even to destroy His visible creation about us.
But His place and His reign are eternally secure.
And so are they who put their trust in Him,
    who live by His precepts,
        and who follow His course for their lives.

94

It is difficult, O God, to understand
how You can ignore Your enemies
or fail to take action against them
as they persist in thwarting Your purposes
and abusing Your children upon this world.
They provoke me to anger, O Lord.
How can You withhold Your vengeance?

Even those of us who name Your name
and sing Your praises
are often indifferent to or careless about
the needs of our fellowmen about us.
We stand indicted, Lord.
Our calloused self-centeredness has perpetuated
the wars and poverty and bigotry
that abound about us.
We don't hate these people, Lord.
We just don't really care about them.

Is it possible, O Lord, that we are Your enemies?
That we are thwarting Your purposes
and abusing Your children upon this world?
We are busy with good works, Lord.
We build churches and send forth missionaries
and establish schools and hospitals
and homes for the elderly.
But we don't like the ghettos, Lord,
or the people who can't speak our language

or don't appreciate our patronizing gifts.
They frighten us when they reach out
for what we have labored for,
our affluence, our respectability,
our right to be wealthy
and comfortable and secure.
Sometimes, Lord, we just don't like people.
Why don't they leave us alone
so we can love and serve You in peace?

Thank You, God, for not pouring out Your wrath
upon those who are disobedient to You.
We have been Your enemies.
Even while we worship
in our comfortable sanctuaries,
we have stood in Your way.
And thank You, God,
because You love even Your enemies
and through Your chastisement
may translate them into sons.

Strike the scales from our eyes, O Lord,
that we may see Your handwriting on the wall
and accept Your chastening love
and return to You in repentance and faith.
Strike the shackles from our hearts and hands
that we may reach out to demonstrate
and to relate Your love
to Your children all about us.

Let us begin this day with singing.
Whether we feel like it or not,
    let us make glad sounds
        and force our tongues to articulate words
           of thanksgiving and praise.

The facts are: God is with us;
    this world and we who live in it are His;
    He loves us;
    He has adopted us as His children;
    we belong to Him.
This makes us valid, worthwhile.
We are truly significant in the eyes of our God,
    irrespective of our human feelings
        or the comments of our critics about us.

This may not be the way we feel this morning,
    but this is the way it is.
We don't need the plaudits of our peers,
    for we have God's stamp of approval.

So let us begin this day with singing
    whether we feel like it or not.
Then we may end this day with praises,
    because we know — and may even feel —
        that we shall forever be
           the objects of God's concern
           and the children of His love.

God is here; God is now!
It is a time for celebration!
Our praises need not be confined to old songs.
Nor need we great organs or massive choirs
        to honor His name.
Let us create new songs of praise to our God.
Let us discover new ways of proclaiming
        His greatness and glory.

The elements about us reflect His majesty.
The roaring sea and all that inhabits it,
        the wind that bends the trees,
        the creatures that fill the air and land,
        the mountains that probe our skies,
        the rivers and lakes that slake our thirst,
        the great planets and stars
            that light up our night—
        all these reveal God's beauty and splendor.
And out of this comes that fashioned
        by man's mind and hand:
            rockets and computers,
            art, architecture, music, literature.

Wherever one turns,
        God's power is manifested,
        God's presence is made apparent.
Let us celebrate His presence
        in our world today.

97

I can't even see the sun this morning.
The coastland fog has blotted out heaven's light,
    and the early hours are cold and damp.
But God is here — in me and around me,
    and I will rejoice in Him.

I hear no angel choirs.
There are no church bells to summon me to worship.
There are only the thunder of four-wheel vehicles
      and the acrid odor of exhaust
    as men rush forth to their unnumbered shrines
      and pursue their avaricious goals.
But God is here, and I will rejoice in Him.

I cannot see the mountains or smell the flowers
    or even hear the song of birds.
I cannot love the people who bustle about me.
I see unhappiness and injustice and depravity.
I hear the ear-grating sounds of pain and complaint.
I feel the stifling pressures that suck me
    into the stream that rushes by my door.
But God is here — in me and around me,
    and I will rejoice in Him.

Our great God does care for His creatures.
He secures forever those who relate to Him.
He is here — in us and around us.
Let us all rejoice in Him!

Men have proclaimed God's praises
throughout the ages.
Now it is our turn to worship the Lord
and to announce God's presence
and His loving concern
for the inhabitants of this world.
His power is as great today as it ever was.
He continues to reign over His universe
and the creatures that move in this world.
He alone is the true God.
He offers to all men His salvation.
He is close to His sons and servants
and fills the hearts of His children with joy.

Now, as His sons and servants,
let us express this joy.
With voice and musical instruments,
with lovely melodies and joyful sounds,
let us proclaim the glory of God.
Let us fill our homes and sanctuaries,
our halls of learning,
our factories and marketplaces,
even the streets of our city,
with sounds of celebration.
God is here; God is now!

99

The Lord does reign over this world!
Even when the earth quakes
     and the fires rage through the canyons
     and floods inundate the lowlands
     and men and their creations are laid low,
   God is Lord and Master over all the earth.

The Lord does reign over this world!
Even when men turn against one another
     and nations are engaged in war
     and violence and injustice are heaped
      ' upon His creatures,
   God is Lord and Master over all the earth.

God's creatures bear the consequences
     of their self-centeredness,
   and this world is distorted by their depravity.
But the Lord forgives those who turn to Him
   and makes them His children and His servants
   and through them seeks to heal
     this world's gaping wounds
     and the hurts that men inflict upon one another.

The Lord relates to those who call upon Him.
The priests and prophets of history
   heard His voice
   and followed in His course for their lives.
His servants and disciples of this hour

155

sense His presence
and communicate His love and grace
to those who reach out for Him.

The Lord does reign over this world!
He is Lord and Master over all the earth!

Break forth
>into exclamations of joy and gladness,
>you who serve the Lord!

God is not dead! He is ever our God!
He made us, we belong to Him;
>we are His sons and servants.
And His love for us never runs out;
>His care and concern for us will go on forever.

Let the world see our manifestations of joy!
Let us lift up our voices in songs of praise
>and surrender our lives
>>as perpetual offerings of thanksgiving!
Let us bless His name forever!

O God, I love those hymns
        that speak of loyalty and justice,
       those prayers for the deprived and oppressed —
     even while I deprive and oppress my fellowmen
     through my apathy and egocentricity.

I embrace the old creeds that tell of Your love
       and the commandments that instruct me
         to reflect that love to others —
     even while I turn inward
     and allow bigotry and prejudice
       to color my relationships
       to those outside my private little club.

I treasure those promises I made in the sanctuary,
       those vows and solemn pledges before the altar —
     even while I flirt with this world's gods
     and bow before man-made shrines.

I decry the distortions of our world,
       the poverty and pain and the indignities
       suffered by multitudes
       of this world's citizens —
     even while I stand aloof
     and wait for man's sorry needs
       to be met by others
     and brazenly oppose those remedies
       which may result in personal deprivation.

I avoid the sinner
    and belittle the proud
    and stand clear of cheaters and liars
    and choose as my companions
      the qualified
    and respected
      members of my society.
And all the while I claim to be Your son
    and to walk in Your ways.

Have mercy upon me, O God,
    for I am a selfish and self-centered creature!

102

Good Lord, where are You?
If You really do exist,
    why don't You come out of hiding and
        do something about this creature in distress?

I am physically weary, I am mentally depressed,
I am spiritually defeated.
I can't eat, can't sleep.
I am like garbage,
    discarded refuse in the back alley;
    like yesterday's newspaper
        shuffled around by the wind.
I feel like some sort of zombi,
    some nonentity,
    some nothing that people,
        if they acknowledge,
    would only curse.
I eat crow and drink gall.
Now even You have tossed me aside
    like some moth-eaten garment
        that no one could possibly want.

But the prophets have proclaimed Your name,
    and the Scriptures declare Your mercy,
    and the old saints pass on Your promises.
You do reign over our world, they say,
    You do show concern
        for the poor clods of this earth.

Good Lord, prove it!
Look down from wherever You are
    on Your creatures wallowing in wretchedness.
Deliver us, O God, set us free!

I must take comfort in Your everlastingness —
    that You who outlive seasons and centuries,
        who have blessed the saints of the past,
      can also care for Your servants
        in this fearful hour.
For Your years have no end,
    nor do the destinies of those who trust in You.

103

My heart is bursting with praises to God;
    every fiber of my being reaches out in rejoicing!
How can I ever forget His many blessings?
    He forgives all my sins;
    He touches my afflictions with healing;
    He snatches me back
      from the gaping jaws of hell;
    He covers me with concern and love;
    He fulfills my deepest desires and gives me
      meaning for life and purpose for living.

God is a God of justice and judgment,
    but He is on the side of those who need His help.
He is angry with those
      who persistently rebel against Him,
    but He pours out His love
      upon those who turn to Him.
He does not give us our just deserts
    or pay us what we well deserve.
He is grieved when we so miserably fail,
    but He quickly draws us to His forgiving heart
      and accepts us just as if it never happened.
He looks with tenderness
      upon His faltering children;
    He knows and understands our fallible natures.

Man by himself is a pitiful picture of weakness.
Now and then one will,

like a streaking meteor,
blaze out across the skies of time,
only to become a smoking cinder
at the end of his short journey.
But those who tie on
to God's loving will and purposes
become the objects
of His eternal mercy and righteousness.

Rejoice with me,
you who are His invisible servants
and you who hear and obey His voice.
Shout His praises,
you who are His children
and you who serve
as His ministers and priests.
There is no time for despair and discouragement.
Whoever and wherever you are,
lift your hearts in praises to God.

104

O Lord, how great and all-powerful You are!
And how beautiful is the world You created
    for our habitation!
Even before man was brought forth from the dust,
    You prepared for him a place
      in which to live and grow.
And everything man saw about him
    reflected the beauty and power
      of the living God.

There was clean air.
Pure water from snowcapped mountains
    flowed through green valleys
    and gathered together to become great lakes.
The skies shone with a million lights.
The land brought forth flowers and fruits
    to delight the eye and palate of God's creature.
And every part of the land
    and the waters that covered the land
    and the skies that looked down upon the land
      were filled with uncountable forms of life;
    the world was vibrant and alive.

Your power and Your beauty were spread
    throughout the universe,
    but it was only upon the heart of man
      that You imprinted Your image.
And this creature,

in his short stay upon this world,
was destined to be Your son and co-worker
in the ever-continuing process of creation.
Your creative activity has never ceased.
It continues in and through the life
of creature man.
Limited and fallible as man is,
his mind and his hands are assigned
to corral Your lifegiving energies
and io direct them in controlling
and replenishing the earth
that life might be given and sustained
throughout the world.

O Lord, how great and all-powerful You are!
And how beautiful is the world You created
for our habitation!

Sisters of Christian Charity
Holy Family Convent and Infirmary
Danville, Pennsylvania 17821

How great is my God,
and how I love to sing His praises!
Whereas I am often frightened
when I think about the future,
and confused and disturbed
by the rapidly changing events about me,
my heart is secured and made glad
when I remember how He has cared for me
throughout the past.

When I was brought forth from my mother's womb,
God's hand was upon me.
Through parents and people who cared,
He loved and sheltered me
and set me upon His course for my life.
Through illness and accident
my God has sustained me.
Around pitfalls and precipices
He has safely led me.
When I became rebellious
and struck out on my own,
He waited patiently for me to return.
When I fell on my face in weakness and failure,
He gently set me upon my feet again.
He did not always prevent me from hurting myself,
but He took me back to heal my wounds.
Even out of the broken pieces of my defeats
He created a vessel of beauty and usefulness.

Through trials and errors, failures and successes,
my God has cared for me.
From infancy to adulthood
He has never let me go.
His love has led me — or followed me —
through the valleys of sorrow
and the highlands of joy,
through times of want
and years of abundance.
He has bridged impassable rivers
and moved impossible mountains.
Sometimes through me,
sometimes in spite of me,
He seeks to accomplish His purposes in my life.

He has kept me through the stormy past;
He will secure and guide me
through the perilous future.
I need never be afraid,
no matter how uncertain
the months or years ahead of me.
How great is my God,
and how I love to sing His praises!

How I praise God today!
How exciting it is to be His son and servant!
What is so amazing to me
    is the manner in which He makes
      hay out of the straw
      and stubble of my feeble efforts
        and foolish errors.

This is the way God deals with all His children.
We have so often fallen away from His love
    and accepted His gifts
      without respect or concern for the Giver.
We spout with gratitude
    when some great deliverance
      has come our way:
    a successful surgery, a return to health,
    a financial bonus, a debt erased,
    a reconciliation with a loved one.
But when the crisis is over and calm is restored,
    we are back to our old tricks,
      walking in our old ways,
      pursuing our self-centered goals,
      with little concern
        about God's way and will for our lives.

We rejoice when God smiles upon us,
    and sound off
      about how good and gracious He is.

But when we meet up with hard times
        or become enslaved
            within the boredom of the daily routine,
        we relapse into grumbling and griping
begin ✓   and act as if God were a million miles away.

How loving and patient is my God!
Even when I fail Him,
        He never fails to love and care for me.
I so often limit Him
        by my inability to really trust Him,
            my unwillingness to obey Him,
        by my apathy, my self-concern,
            or my pursuit of the foolish
                goals and ambitions of this life.
And yet my God never ceases to pursue me,
        to draw me back into His circle of love,
        and to carry out His purposes
            even through the failures and defeats
                of my life.

How I praise God today! *for this gift of Sae,*
How I pray that He may find pleasure
        in my love for Him!

107

Those who have experienced
    the redemption of God
  and know what it means
    to be reconciled to Him
  ought to dedicate their lives to serving Him
  and their voices to proclaiming
    to the world His loving grace.

Some of you have known
  the meaning of emptiness and loneliness
You have drunk from many wells
  and sipped honey from many flowers
  and stumbled into many blind alleys
    in your search for fulfillment.
But your hearts remained empty and unsatisfied.
Then you faced up to God
  and His claim on you,
  and you discovered purpose and objective
    for your lives.
Don't keep it to yourselves!
Tell it to the world!
Proclaim in word and deed
  the wonderful works of a loving God.
Let others know that He is able
  to fill their emptiness and satiate their hunger.

Some of you have endured
  long nights of suffocating darkness.

You know well the dregs of depression,
    the power of obsession,
        the clutch of despair and frustration on your souls.
You fell on your faces in defeat,
    and no one seemed to care.
Then in desperation you cried out
        to God in your misery;
    and He flooded your lives with light and hope.
Thank God! It is by His eternal love
    that you are delivered.
Tell others about His power to deliver them
    from that which binds them or blinds them.

Some of you have followed
    sin's cruel consequences
        into the crucible of sickness and pain.
You were led to the very brink of destruction.
Then you turned to God in your great distress,
    and He touched you with His healing
        and delivered you from your afflictions.
Rejoice in God! Let your praises ascend to Him!
Proclaim His healing grace
    to others who may be ready to listen.

Some of you have set out in joyous abandon
    to find your happiness
        in the streets and market-places of the great city.
But you became lost and disillusioned and afraid.
The exciting city became a devouring monster
    that threatened to dehumanize and destroy you.
You cried out for help,
    and you found that God was there

among its milling masses.
He restored courage to your hearts
and meaning to your lives.
You discovered purpose
and validity and significance
in the loving acceptance of your God.
Let the city's multitudes hear
about your discovery!
Let them know that God is near
that they may rejoice
in His everlasting and ever-present love.
It is the lack of God in a person's life
that dries him up and turns him into dust.
It is God's presence and acceptance
that turns on the lights
and floods the dark corridors that lead nowhere
and transforms them into warm rooms
wherein one may live
in joy and fulfillment.
It is the acknowledgment of a loving God
that makes the forbidding city
a place to live in
and its God-fearing inhabitants
glowing reflections of His eternal concern.

Great God, be it city street or mountaintop,
may it become my pulpit
from which to proclaim Your praises,
and my workbench
from which to transmit Your love
to the lives of lonely men.

My heart is glad today, O God,
    and I am determined to serve You!
I celebrate Your presence.
I glory in Your love for me.
I sing Your praises
    and yearn to proclaim Your loving concern to all.

The people I travel with have little feeling for You.
They act as if You do not exist.
They are empty.
Their lives have little meaning or purpose.
They bounce about in a vacuum,
    the deepest longings of their hearts unfulfilled.

I know to whom I belong,
    and I know where I am going.
I know that You are my Lord
    and that You will accompany me
        as I walk the streets of the city and
            mingle with its groping inhabitants.

I pray, O Lord, that You will use me,
    that through my fumbling efforts
        You will touch some soul with healing and love.

My heart is glad today, O God.
Grant that I may communicate to others
    some measure of this eternal joy.

109

O God, I have been taught to believe
    that You are God over our world.
It has been dinned into my ears
    by the preachers of my youth,
    by parents, teachers, and self-appointed apostles.
"God holds the reins," they say.
"He will have the last word," they claim.

I've honestly tried to believe it.
And with tongue in cheek
    I've sounded off to others
        about Your power and Your promises.
Maybe they sensed my incredulity.
It may be that they just habitually accepted
    or unthinkingly nodded assent
        to my platitudes and pronouncements.
How can I really believe in Your omnipotence
    unless I look the other way
        when tragedy befalls
        or close my eyes to the agony and ugliness
            on all sides of me?

I cannot believe You inflict pain on Your creatures.
I realize that our suffering is most often
    the consequences of our own selfishness.
But what about the babies born
        with two strikes against them?
        the grisly slaughter on battlefield, highways?

the destruction of thousands when the earth
     shifts and breaks up under them?
the pressures and indignities
     forced upon minority races?
What about this, O God?
How can I explain this to my skeptical friends
     or even to myself?

Is it possibly true, O God,
     that You really are not omnipotent?
     that this fractured world is not
          in the palm of Your hand?
     that Your great power is limited
          in respect to this distorted planet
               and its sin-ridden inhabitants?

O God, the basis of all being,
     my ultimate and eternal concern,
     I know that You are not floating out there
          over and beyond our ball of clay.
You are in our world.
You are amongst Your creatures,
     inscrutable, indefinable,
          great in majesty and splendor.
You bring beauty out of ugliness.
Out of the ashes of our sickness and suffering
     You bring forth new creations.
I shall never want to define You, O God,
     for I cannot worship what I comprehend.
But I pray for Your grace to stand firm
          even amid my nagging doubts
          and to praise You in time of adversity.

God spoke to me today.
He broke through my childish doubts
    with words of comfort and assurance.
"Hang in there; sit tight;
       stick to My course for your life," He said,
    "I will not let you down."

He reminded me of how He cared for past saints,
    how He watched over them and kept them
       through their hours of suffering
        and uncertainty.
He reviewed for me my own life,
    His loving concern through the days of my youth.
He restated for me my commission and appointment,
    His trust in me as His servant
       in this sorry world.
He reiterated His gracious promises to stand by me,
    to empower and support me
       in the conflicts that await me.

I know that God is with me today —
    Just as surely as He was with His saints of old.
I have neither to fear nor to doubt
    the eternal love and presence of my Lord.

My heart is full today.
I am so grateful
    for all that God has done for me.
I need but crawl out of my corner
        of depression and self-pity
      and look around me to see
        how great my God is.
I cannot see Him,
      but I can see the works of His hands.
He is a merciful and loving God.
How tenderly He deals with those
    whose hearts are open to Him!
He is a righteous and faithful God.
His promises and precepts are forever.
He is a majestic and powerful God.
He created me and sustains me day by day.
He is a forgiving God.
He takes me back to His loving heart
    when I go astray.
He is in this world today.
And those who recognize and accept His presence
    are building on foundations
        that are eternally secure.
How grateful I am to my God today!

What about the man who trusts in God
    and is committed to His will and purposes?

He is a man who is rich indeed.
Even amid the circumstances of poverty,
    the wealth and blessings of God
        are within his reach.
He is a man with purpose and meaning in his life.
Even amid the disorder and void
      of this temporal existence,
    he is aware of God's concern and love for him.
He is a man who walks unafraid.
The threats of violence or prophecies of doom
    do not detract from his validity
      nor alter his course.
He is a man who relates to his fellow beings.
He identifies with them
      in their sorrows and complaints
    and shares with them his life and his gifts.

He is the man who is truly happy
    and through whom our God is working out
      His purposes in this world today.

How great and glorious is our God!
From hour to hour, from day to day
    our lives ought to overflow
      with praise and gratitude.
It is amazing, even fantastic,
    how our God permeates every facet of our lives
      and can work out His purposes through them
        despite our human faults and failures.

He creates beauty out of the dust
    of our fallen natures.
Out of the ashes of our failures
    He brings forth meaning and purpose.
He exalts the humble and enriches the poor.
He transforms our weaknesses
    into channels of strength.
Our emptiness becomes
    a vessel of His fullness,
    our spiritual poverty
      the basis for His eternal grace.
Our errors and mistakes
    are stepping-stones to success.
Our defeats are but incidents
    on the road to victory.

But this is God's doing, not ours.
How great and glorious is our God!

114 and 115

We fear, O God, for our country
    and the tragic indifference that is demonstrated
    in respect to You and Your purposes.
We have built great shrines and memorials
    in Your honor.
We have established innumerable religions
    that presume to glorify and serve You.
We have respectfully imprinted Your name
    upon our coins
    and properly credited You
    in our founding principles.
Our leaders generally call on You to guide them
    in the most critical decisions
    they must make.
A remnant of our populace gathers occasionally
    to sing Your praises and profess its faith.
There are even special days
    when we count our blessings
    and conduct services of thanksgiving.

But the shrines we build do not always glorify You.
They often become soundproof fortresses
    that blot out the sounds of suffering
    which echo throughout the world about them.
Our numerous religions turn into vain attempts
    to box You into man-made ideas
    and concepts of divinity.
The coins which bear Your name are dedicated

to the pursuit of our selfish ambitions
and the acquisition of material wealth.
Our founding principles are interpreted in ways
that benefit the powerful and oppress the weak.
Our laws sometimes contradict and oppose Your law
in respect to the consciences and convictions
of Your children.
Our leaders call upon You to bless their intentions
rather than to reveal Your plans
in the government of men.
And those who do gather to sing Your praises
are seldom committed to anyone or anything
unless it is comfortable and convenient
for their purposes.

And yet, O Lord, we pray
that You will not give us up.
We have selfishly clutched at Your great blessings
and abused the wealth You have put
into our hands.
We have gathered for ourselves
while countless millions
of this world's creatures have died
with their needs unfulfilled.
We have foolishly ignored You to worship the things
that have come from Your hands.
We confess our rebelliousness and selfishness,
O Lord,
and pray that You will spare us.
Spare us, in order that you might renew us
and save us
and use us to channel Your blessings

to Your children in every land.
You dealt mercifully with Your ungrateful children
throughout history.
We pray that You will deal patiently and lovingly
with us,
that You will transform our words into actions
and our shallow platitudes into genuine praises
that will glorify and serve You
in all the world.

116

I know that God is here.
I know this because,
     my soul bare and body naked before Him,
    He looked upon me with love
      and responded to my cry for help.

There was a time when I didn't care!
I was not aware of any particular need for Him.
But then I hit bottom.
Death itself reached out to embrace me.
There was no one else to turn to.
I cried out to God in my desperation.
I could almost feel His invisible hand
     encircle me and draw me to Himself.

Now I am convinced.
God is here, and I shall trust Him forever.
I will no longer wait for pain or suffering
     to drive me to Him.
I will walk in His course for my life.
I am committed to His purposes,
     and I intend to carry out that commitment.

I can never repay God for His ever-present love.
I can only dedicate my life to praising Him
     and to serving Him wherever I may be.
I am His servant and His son; I shall love Him forever.
I shall proclaim to all the world: "God is in our midst."

117 and 118

O God, I am thoroughly frightened when I see
    the things that are happening around me.
And when I dare to peer into the future,
    I become very nervous as I consider
        what may happen to me and my world.

I do remember Your many promises.
I keep telling myself:
      "With the Lord on my side
        I do not have to be afraid;
      what can man do unto me?"
But when I see the old foundations crumbling
      and the old certainties
      and securities giving way,
    I feel as if I am falling with no one
      to catch me,
    or that my ship has broken loose
      from its anchor, leaving me
        at the mercy of a tempestuous sea.

Our world has slipped its moorings:
      our population threatens to overwhelm us;
      our waste products are about to smother us;
      our modern weapons are capable
        of obliterating us.
Because we are incapable of loving and living
      for one another,
    we are about to be destroyed

by our own self-centeredness
and to turn the beautiful world You have given us
   into a wasted and desolate planet.
It all seems so unreal,
     and I feel so small and insignificant
       in such a world.
And sometimes it seems, O God,
     that even You have left us to our own devices
       and have given us up for lost.
Or, I wonder, are You about to wind up history?
Is Your purpose for our world
   about to be consummated?

You do speak to my fears, O Lord.
You offer no guarantees
     about the future of the world,
    but You have assured me that my status
     as Your beloved child is eternal.
Whatever happens to my world,
    You will never let me go.
You have set me free from fear
   and will keep me safe and secure
     through all the storms
       that rage about me.
You are my God,
    whatever happens to the world about me,
   and I will celebrate Your love forever.

185

Sisters of Christian Charity
Holy Family Convent and Infirmary
Danville, Pennsylvania 17821

119

O God, I want so very much to please You,
    to walk in Your ways
    and to carry out Your purposes.
There is nothing as important to me
    as being in the center of Your will
    and living within Your design for my life.

While others may find their fulfillment
    in the acquisition of wealth
      or the accumulation of things,
    in doing something better than everyone else,
      or in the plaudits of their peers,
    my foremost desire is
      to be the object of Your love
      and to be Your child and servant forever.

Not only have You fashioned me with Your hands,
    O Lord,
    and created me for Your purposes.
You have stamped Your image upon my heart.
Therefore my deepest longings are met only in You
    and in the dedication of my life
      to the accomplishment of Your objectives.

How can I live a life that is pleasing to You,
    O Lord?
My instincts are earthbound.
The ephemeral delights of this life

tantalize and tempt me.
My insatiable longings
and desperate attempts to please You
are thwarted by the innumerable enemies
of my soul.
I fail so often to do what I really want to do,
to attain what I strive for,
to grasp what I reach for,
and I fall back in shame
and am flattened in despair.

You do forgive me when I fail, O Lord,
and You put me upon my feet again.
You have promised to strengthen me
and to sustain me in my daily conflicts.
Now I pray for the wisdom to discern Your will
and the grace to carry it out
in the difficult days before me.

You have shown me how much You love me, Lord;
now show me how to love You.
Your standards for me are clear.
I am to translate Your love into terms
that others can comprehend,
to demonstrate it before my fellowmen about me.
I can truly love You only inasmuch as I proceed
to love Your children in this world.
I can serve You only as I commit my life to service
on behalf of my brothers and sisters.
I can offer sacrifices to You only by way
of the altar of my neighbor's need.
This is Your law, Your standard,

Your design and will for my life.
This is the way in which I will be pleasing to You.

I do love You, O God,
	and Your will for me is the delight of my heart.
I have a sincere love for many people
		who cross my path,
	and I rejoice in the privilege of serving them.
And yet, O Lord, there are so many people
	whom I do not love.
The demons of bigotry and apathy
	and jealousy and selfishness
		plague my soul and numb my sensitivities
		and stay my hand from reaching out
			to help my fellowman.
I sin against You when I sin against them,
	and I need to be restored and renewed
		by Your loving touch.

How I praise You, O Lord,
	because You love me even when I fail
		to respond in loving obedience!
Whereas I cannot comprehend You,
	You do understand me,
	and You continue to hold me
		within Your loving embrace.
While I fall short of my sincere intentions
		to abide within Your will for me,
	Your promises are eternally secure,
	and You tenderly and patiently
		rekindle the fires within me and empower me
			to do that which I cannot do by myself.

I love You, O God,
and I gladly accept Your will and purpose
for my life.
Now bless me and guide me
and grant me the grace
to walk within that will and purpose
and have the joy of knowing
that I am pleasing to You.

120

I am distressed, O Lord,
    by the attitudes and actions of those
      who claim to honor Your name
        and to live within Your purposes.

They don't really listen to Your Word.
They appear to be following some other god
    or are simply taking the path
      of least resistance.
They assume that their wishes are Your will,
    that the crowd they travel with
    or the nations that govern them
      are righteously carrying out Your objectives
        irrespective of their ungodly
        means and methods.

How long, O Lord, must I dwell
    in a world that breeds violence
    and amongst people that engage in war?

Teach me, O God, how to be a peacemaker,
    how to confront violence with love,
    how to courageously and patiently promote
      Your will and Your Word
        among the hostile and angry masses.

121

Where should I look for help in my need?
To majestic mountain peaks that probe our skies
    or to giants of industry that hem in our cities?
To satellites that circle our world
    or to computers that store up our knowledge?

The answer to my problems
        and the fulfillment of my needs
    must come from God Himself,
        from Him who created skies and mountains
            and man to dwell in their midst.
He is a great God who knows our every desire,
    whose watchful eye is upon us night and day.
We can make no move without His knowledge.
His concern for His children is constant;
    His love for them is eternal.

And thus the Lord will keep you,
Shielding you from the forces of evil
    as a shade tree shields you
        from the rays of the blazing sun.

He does care for you,
    and He will fight with you
        against the enemies of your soul.
Whether you be coming or going,
    He knows the course you take,
        and He will go before you.

122 and 123

How good it is to enter the sanctuary of the Lord!
I know that God is not confined
    within man's four-walled creations,
   nor is He attached to altars and brass symbols.
And yet, in the beauty and quietness of God's house
    I find His presence very real and fulfilling.

God is with me and about me
    even as I make my way
      through the concrete and steel jungles
        of the cold and unfriendly city.

He is present even behind the anonymous faces
    of the rushing crowds elbowing their way
      to their respective destinations.
I find Him in the hearts and lives of His children
    who infiltrate the urban masses
    and who are running His errands
      and fulfilling His purposes
        in the course of their daily duties.
I cannot outrun or evade my God.
He goes before me and follows closely behind me.
He will keep me and sustain me wherever I am.

And yet I rejoice as I enter His sanctuary
    and mingle with those who honor His name
      and seek His grace.

There, shielded from the screaming tensions
and ear-splitting sounds of the city,
in the company of those who love one another,
I happily open my heart
to the loving mercy of God.

124 and 125

What cowards we are,
    we who claim to be the sons of God!
How insipid is our faith
    in an insecure and faithless world!

The pressures are increasing.
The old props are falling away.
Many of the old traditions and standards
    we held so dear
    are no longer relevant
    in our rapidly changing society.
Even the proclamations and exhortations,
    the prophecies and promises,
    that excited and supported us in our youth
    sound hollow and empty, frightfully inadequate
    in these times in which we live.
The little boxes we wrapped around our God
    are breaking up;
    we can no longer hold on to Him
    in our expanding, exploding universe.

Though we cannot hold on to God,
    He does hold on to us.
Those who trust in the true God are more secure
    than the great mountains that rise
    above the clouds that cover us.
Though everything changes about us,
    our great God cannot be changed.

Though the sands may shift around us,
>   even our institutions and governments
>   and the ideals and aspirations of men,
>   our great God is not subject to the impermanence
>   of our temporal world.
Though the storm sweeps in upon us,
>   our relationship to our loving God is forever.

What cowards we are, we who claim to be
>   the sons of God!
We don't have to be afraid.
Let us have faith in God!

126

Let us begin this day by rejoicing!
Let us acknowledge our Lord's love and concern
    and allow our bodies to break forth
       into happy hilarity!
Let us give our nerves and muscles
    the healthy exercise of laughter!
The Lord has done such wonderful things for us;
    let us be glad!

The day before us is uncertain.
We know not what we will encounter on our way.
While we rejoice with those who rejoice,
    we shall also weep with those who suffer.
While we may be surprised by ecstasy,
    we may also pass through corridors of darkness.
Wherever we go, we go forth as sons and servants
      of the living God,
    and we go forth to touch the lives of men
      with His healing love.
Let us begin this day with rejoicing,
    and return to our homes with gladness!

127 and 128

Man's struggle for significance
    apart from God's will and purposes
      is in vain.
Man builds homes and institutions;
    he acquires property and possessions;
    he crowds the cities with the clutter
      of questionable achievements;
    he fills the better part of every day
      with self-centered activities;
    he pushes and prods in an anxiety-ridden quest
      for some ephemeral treasure;
    he strives incessantly to get to the top.
And all the while worth and value
    are within him or very close to him.
They are the precious gifts of God
    that come in some measure to all men.

There are visible evidences of a man's worth:
    the children he begets,
    the beloved mate that brings him joy,
    the ability to supply
      his own and his family's needs
      through his daily labors.
But even beyond this and long before this,
    a man's true worth was established
      by God Himself.

129

O God, I get awfully tired of static.
I am fed up with the flack that comes my way
      from those I am trying to serve.
It seems that they suspect or misinterpret
      or question my motives or authority
            in respect to everything I do or say.
I think people enjoy putting me down.
I just can't get them off my back.

Do I have to perpetually live
      with this sort of thing, O Lord?
What about this joy that is promised to those
      who are Your servants and ministers?

Forgive me for my unworthy thoughts, O Lord.
Overlook my vicious complaints,
      and so fill my heart with Your love
            that I will respond in love
                  even toward those who cannot love me.
Enable me, O Lord, to find my joy in You
      and to reflect that joy to the unresponsive,
            reactionary, disagreeable people
                  who do not like me very much.

130

O God, tonight I seek for You
> out of a heart full of guilt
>> and a mind full of bewilderment
>> and frustration.

You have heard me before
> and responded with grace and mercy.

Now I seek You again.

I know I am guilty, O God;
But if You kept account
> of man's failings and fallings,
> no one could ever face You again.

I reach for You
> because You look with loving mercy
>> upon my wretched soul.

You will accept me and forgive me
> and reinstate me in Your purposes.

It is no wonder that I return
> again and again to God.

I long for His forgiveness and acceptance
> more than the night watchman longs
>> for the dawn of day.

Thus I plead with you to focus your faith on God.
You will find love there—and salvation.
And He will cleanse you of your sins
> and restore you to His loving heart.

131

O God, I have failed
>because I expected too much of myself.

I have fallen
>because I focused too much on success
>>and reckoned too little with my own humanity.

It is time that I still my restless heart
>and quiet my overambitious spirit.

It is far better that we center our aspirations
>on God and His will for our lives.

132

We remember, O Lord,
    those past saints who suffered sorely
      on Your behalf.
In obedience to You they endured persecution —
    even torture and death.
In their heroic determination to live by Your will
      and to remain in Your course for their lives,
    they proclaimed and demonstrated Your Word
      to this world's masses.

We remember, O Lord,
    and we are ashamed of our insipid faith,
      our cowardice,
        our fear of offending those with power over us
          and of being despised by our fellowmen.

Make us aware, O Lord,
    of Your children who even today
      are suffering for their faith,
    who, even in our great country,
      have the courage to place Your will
        above the laws of the state
      and are subjected to
        the indignities of imprisonment,
        the scorn of their peers,
        and even the compassionless criticisms
      of many of us who honor Your name.

We confess, O Lord,
  our lack of courage and understanding.
We pray for Your blessing upon those who suffer,
  that You will not forget them
    in their hour of trial,
  and that You will not turn Your face from them
    in their lonely hours of doubt and pain.

Visit them with joy; empower them with Your Spirit;
  watch over and care for them.
May the influence of their courageous convictions
  shake us out of our lethargy,
  move us from the fringes of fear and indecision
    into the center of Your will,
  and endue us with the grace
    to carry on Your purposes
      in scorn of the consequences
      that may come to our lives.

133 and 134

O God, how precious it is for us
and how pleasing it must be to You
when Your sons and servants learn
how to live and work together in unity!

It is in the measure that we do this
that we begin to resemble You
and to carry out most effectively Your purposes
in our disjointed and discordant world.

Come, let us together bless His name,
rejoice in His loving concern for us,
declare His worth to all creatures,
and walk in obedience to His will.

It is the same God who made heaven and earth
and all of us who dwell therein.
Let us worship and serve Him together.

135

Despite the depressing conditions of our world
    and the distortions of our society,
      or even the problems and conflicts of our lives,
    let us take time to praise the Lord.

We who gather for services of worship,
    let us come together to celebrate God's presence
      and to praise Him for His great gifts.
As we find our place in our workaday world,
    let us begin by praising the Lord.
When we meet with our family and friends,
    let us unite our voices in praises to the Lord.
The farmer who labors alone with the soil and seed
    can praise that God
      who brings forth the fruit.
The city dweller who mingles with the masses
    that impersonally jostle him
  and works amid the tall structures
    that belittle him
  can praise that God who knows
    and loves him forever.
Without our God to praise and worship and serve,
    there is no real purpose in life,
      no meaning, no identity, and no reason
        for existing in this cold, calculating world.
You who are on beds of pain,
    even you have reason to praise the Lord.
You who are left to die in homes for the aged,

you, too, can find purpose
    in praising the Lord.
When you feel you are forgotten,
    your loving God never forgets.
When you are tired and lonely,
    your great God will never leave your side.

Those people who have no God to praise,
    who neglect to relate
        to their Creator and Redeemer,
    are like creatures wandering in darkness.
They focus upon the fitful, fleeing things
    of this life.
Like butterflies over a flower bed,
    they flutter from blossom to blossom,
        getting their honey wherever they can.
Then they return to their beds
    only to await the meaningless existence
        of another day.

God is available—to be recognized and praised.
He has reached out to His lost children
    to lovingly draw them to Himself.
He gives them identity and purpose,
    a name and a goal,
    and makes them
        eternally secure and significant.

Let us praise the Lord!
He makes our lives and our living,
    every hour and every day, truly worthwhile;
    and we belong to Him forever.

Thank You, God,
>for all these things that reveal Your love.
Thank You for the heavens that cover us,
>for the earth beneath our feet,
>for the sun in the day and the stars of the night,
>for the snow and the rains
>>and the rivers and the lakes,
>for mountains and valleys and trees and flowers.

Thank You, God,
>for those people who demonstrate Your love.
Thank You for those great men who followed You
>>throughout history,
>for the priests and prophets
>>and apostles and ministers,
>for doctors and teachers and mothers and fathers
>>and painters and musicians and writers
>>and farmers and laborers and clerks,
>for those men and women who accepted Your love
>>and dedicated their lives
>>>to loving their fellowman.

Thank You, God,
>for choosing me to be one of Your people,
>for calling me and equipping me to communicate
>>Your love to my world about me.
Thank You, God.

137

How grateful we are, O God,
 for our great country
 for the blessings You lavish upon our land!
How concerned we are, O God,
 that our very nation may become our god
 and that we worship the gifts
 rather than the Giver!

Is it possible, O God,
 that our laws may circumvent Your will?
 that our freedom may place chains on others?
 that our wealth impoverish someone?
 that our power may come
 by way of another's weakness?
 that our enemies may be those
 who are obedient to You?
Dare we pray, O God,
 that You take away those things that come
 between us and You?
 that You raise up men who will oppose
 those institutions and those citizens
 who carelessly, even unconsciously,
 equate patriotism with allegiance to You?

We do pray, O God,
 that our nation be restored to Your objectives
 and that Your children who abide in this land
 dedicate their lives to You and Your purposes.

I am exceedingly grateful, O Lord,
>for You have heard my cries and complaints,
>and You responded with mercy and strength.
Now my life is overflowing with thanksgiving,
>and my mouth is filled with Your praises.

If only the leaders of our disjointed world
>>would listen to Your words
>>and direct their people in accord with Your will,
>they would then know the meaning of peace,
>and they would rejoice in the ways of God.

You have not shielded me
>>from the pains of trouble
>>>or the ravages of conflict,
>but You have kept me
>>even amid sorrow and suffering.
You take my side against the enemies of my soul,
>and You will not allow them to destroy me.

Thus I know You will fulfill Your purpose for my life.
Your love and mercy is everlasting;
>You will not let me go.

139

O God, You know me inside and out,
    through and through.
Everything I do,
        every thought that flits through my mind,
        every step I take,
        every plan I make,
        every word I speak,
    You know, even before these things happen.
You know my past;
    You know my future.
Your circumventing presence covers my every move.
Your knowledge of me sometimes comforts me,
        sometimes frightens me;
    but always it is far beyond my comprehension.

There is no way to escape You, no place to hide.
If I ascend to the heights of joy,
    You are there before me.
If I am plunged into the depths of despair,
    You are there to meet me.
I could fly to the other side of our world
    and find You there to lead the way.
I could walk into the darkest of nights,
        only to find You there
            to lighten its dismal hours.

You were present at my very conception.
You guided the molding of my unformed members

within the body of my mother.
Nothing about me, from beginning to end,
    was hid from Your eyes.
How frightfully, fantastically wonderful it all is!

May Your all-knowing, everywhere-present Spirit
    continue to search out my feelings and thoughts.
Deliver me
    from that which may hurt or destroy me,
    and guide me along the paths of love and truth.

140

O God, deliver our nation and our world
from those men in positions of authority
who resort to violence
to carry out their objectives.
They sweet-talk us into believing
they are acting in our interests,
and brainwash us into blind,
flag-waving allegiance,
until we march by their side
into bloody wars that decimate and destroy
our brothers and sisters
in the family of man.

Deliver all of us, O Lord,
from the notion that anything of value or worth
can be obtained by hostile or violent actions.

Our God is on the side of those who are afflicted.
He will justly deal with men of violence,
and show His mercy upon the victims
of their obscene actions.

Help us, O Lord,
even at the risk of our lives and well-being,
to overcome hate with love
and to be peacemakers in a world
that is so racked and distorted
by the atrocities of war.

141

O God, I come to You in sorrow and shame.
I spoke up in my own defense today
    and uttered words that knifed their way
      into the heart of my friend,
    and this created a great rift between us.
I would never raise my hand to strike him,
    but the tongue is more destructive than the fist,
    and I hurt that one whom I love.

Heal the hurt of my friend, O Lord,
    and heal the sickness within my heart
      that forced my foolish tongue
        into such irresponsible actions.

I come to claim Your loving mercy.
I pray, as well, that you grant my friend
    the grace to forgive me.
May Your Spirit who abides in my heart
    curb and control my rebellious tongue
    and teach me to speak words
      that give life and promote love
        in the hate-ridden world about me.

142

I direct my cries to the Lord.
Out of the ear-piercing sounds and
      ceaseless turmoil of this concrete jungle
    I speak God's name.
For my heart is deeply troubled and depressed,
    and I feel weary and faint.

I am confused and lost.
I cannot find my way.
The nameless faces that flit by
    take no notice of me.
No one knows my name,
    and no one cares.

I turn to You, O God.
You have heard me before,
    and You responded to my cries.
Perhaps even amid the frustrating activity
      and crowded streets of the great city
    You can hear the cries of a lonely child.

O God, deliver me from my prison of loneliness.
Turn my cries of distress
    into proclamations of joy.
Direct my steps into the fellowship
    of others who love and serve You.

143

It was another one of those days, Lord,
    when I should have stayed in bed.
Everything I attempted to do was destined for failure.
I honestly tried to show concern for my fellowman
    but got cold shoulders in return.
I tried to speak words of comfort,
    and they were thrown right back into my teeth.
I wanted to do well at my job,
    but it seemed I just got in everybody's way.

Sometimes it just isn't worth it, Lord,
    and I wonder if it isn't time to fold up
        and shove off in search of greener pastures.
I want desperately to be a success,
    to add points to my score,
    or to get commended now and then.
But this didn't happen today, Lord,
    and it happens so seldom, I wonder what's wrong.
Am I following Your course for my life,
    or am I just muddling through without design?

I need You, God, more now than ever before.
And if I don't get some special lift,
    some sense of Your support and encouragement,
    I will go right down the tube.

Come closer, O Lord, that I may hear again
    Your voice of comfort and concern.

144

O God, it is difficult to understand
how You can regard man with such high regard
and show him so much concern.
His years upon this earth are so few.
He is little more than a wisp of wind
in the time and space of Your great universe.

You created him as the object of Your love —
only to see him turn from You
to play with his foolish toys.
You tried to teach him to love his fellowman —
only to see him express his fear
and suspicion and hate
through cruel acts of violence and war.
You showered upon him Your abundant gifts —
only to see him make them his ultimate concern.

Still You continue to love him
and seek incessantly to save him
from destroying himself and the world
You have placed in his hands.
Even while he rejects You,
You reach out to draw him back to Yourself.
Even while he suffers the painful consequences
of his rank rebelliousness,
You offer to him Your healing
and demonstrate Your desire
to restore him to love and joy.

And when he finally turns to You,
   he finds You waiting for him,
      ready to forgive his sins and to reunite him
         to Your life and purposes once more.

That man who returns to his God is happy indeed!
He will forever be the object
   of God's love and blessings.

145

God is here—let's celebrate!
Let us enlist our lives in perpetual celebration
      over God's goodness and greatness.
Let us announce to the world God's presence
      and proclaim His loving concern for all men.

How compassionate He is over all He has created,
      how tender toward His failure-fraught creatures!
He will not cop out on His promises to us.
His blessings are not reserved only for those
      who fit obediently into His design for them.
He is just—and He is forgiving.
He gently picks up those who have fallen
      and restores them to sonship and servanthood.
He sustains those who are wavering in weakness
      and grants them His grace and strength.
He reaches into the void of empty lives
      and enriches and fulfills their hungry hearts.
He is near enough to hear our every cry,
    to sense our every need,
    to grant us whatever is necessary
    to make us happy and productive
      as we seek to follow and to serve Him.
How incomparably glorious is our great God!
May our mouths articulate and our lives demonstrate
      His ever-present love for all His creatures.
Let us celebrate
      the eternal mercy and goodness of our God.

146

Praise God!
As long as I have breath in my body,
    I will praise God!

Don't pin your hopes on the genius of man.
His ultimate end is the same as yours,
    and he becomes once more
        like the dust from which he came.

That person is secure
    who draws his strength from God.
He who created the earth and all upon it,
He is He who can heal the wounds
    and mend the fractures of our disjointed world.
He can break the bonds of obsession
    and pierce man's stupor with visions of truth.
He tenderly reaches out
      to those who are oppressed
    and reveals His concern
      for those who are lost and lonely.
He watches over His own
    while the paths of the godless
      lead to their own destruction.

This is the God who cannot die!
Praise God!
Amen!

147 through 150

How good it is to celebrate God's presence
    and to sing His praises throughout each day!
We celebrate what He has done for man
      through history:
    His creation of our world
      and the sun and the moon
      and the unnumbered stars
        that light up our universe;
    His creatures that swim and crawl
      and walk and fly upon our planet;
    His children destined to enjoy
      these great gifts about them.
We praise Him for dealing with creature man:
    through His blessings heaped upon him;
      His revelations through signs and wonders;
      His tender love and gentle concern
        in His caring for him.
We praise Him for His devoted servants:
    who communicated His Word;
    who performed His miracles;
    who brought His healing to men's hurts.
We celebrate His continued blessings to our world:
    the flowers that bloom in glorious color;
    the rains that freshen the earth;
    the birds that fill the air with song.
We give thanks for His perpetual love:
    His forgiveness of men's sin;
    His pursuit of those who run from Him;

221

His reaching out to heal them
and to draw them to Himself.

We call upon all men to praise the Lord:
those who preach to proclaim His love;
those who sing to glorify His name;
those who can shout or whistle
or write or paint
or dance or play musical instruments
or pound on drums or ring bells
to join in celebrating
the majesty of our great and loving God.